D1488943

Taxes for Online Sellers

Taxes for Online Sellers

A How-To Guide for Individuals on Federal Tax for Internet Sales

Simon Elisha

gingersnapbooks

Cover photograph by: Artistic Spaces, www.artisticspacespublishing.com
Cover design by: John Baldwin, www.FPStudio.com, St. Albans, WV

VERSION 2.2

ISBN 10: 0-9796328 -0-3
ISBN 13: 978-0-9796328-0-8

Library of Congress Control Number: 2007903451
Library of Congress Subject Headings:
1. Small business—Taxation—Law and Legislation—United States
2. Self-Employed—Taxation—Law and Legislation—United States
3. Electronic Commerce—Taxation—Law and Legislation—United States—Popular Works

Published by: g i n g e r s n a p b o o k s
(An imprint of Artistic Spaces Publishing)
P.O. Box 330703
Murfreesboro, TN 37133-0703

Printed in the United States of America.

Disclaimer

Special thanks to:

Those who allowed me to ramble on about taxes 24/7, supported my vision, read and offered feedback on the book, and after all of that, still love me anyway.

Dedicated to: My father, the leader of my band.

Contents

Preface

Whether it's Amazon, eBay, or your own website, you put a few things online to sell. You possibly saw the late night infomercials about making millions. More likely, however, you knew someone who made a little money by putting their old sweater on eBay, and thought you'd give it a try.

You were shocked at the things people were willing to buy. You were addicted. Not only did you empty your closets, but cleaned out your children's rooms, as well. Before long, you were actually purchasing discounted or yard sale items to resell for profit. Suddenly, you had a business.

This is how I began as an online seller. By the middle of yard sale season, I knew I'd better start keeping some receipts and records. I worried about the tax implications of my newfound income. I had questions about recording and claiming certain expenses. (Don't even get me started about valuing my inventory!) Online message boards weren't much help. I knew I'd need to seek the expertise of a tax professional.

Though I filed my first Schedule C sixteen years ago, and have gotten quite familiar with self-employment tax laws, I am no tax expert. The following information was compiled as a guide to help other online sellers, like myself. Though the guidelines have been thoroughly researched, they are not intended to be used as your sole resource. Nor is it a comprehensive tax guide. Every taxpayer will have individual circumstances beyond the scope of this book. I have tried to focus on the things most common to the majority of online sellers. Please seek further advice from a tax professional.

Introduction

Future of Taxes for Selling Online

According to the Census Bureau of the Department of Commerce, total retail e-commerce sales for 2006 were estimated at 108.7 billion dollars, an increase of 23.5% from 2005. eBay alone currently claims 97 million users. Though all sellers are supposed to report their income, it is obvious, given the numbers, a great percentage of people don't.

The IRS has set its sights on online sellers not reporting their income. The IRS is currently able to subpoena records from third parties, such as eBay or Paypal, about your income if they suspect foul play. The 2008 proposed federal tax budget would require brokers to collect your Social Security number and report your sales to the IRS on a Form 1099 if sales surpass 100 transactions or more than $5000 annually. Currently, eBay and other online venues aren't considered brokers, but an advisory group for the IRS recommended including online auctions under the definition of brokers. It is certain your online earnings will be reported to the IRS by online selling venues. The question has simply been when.

In the future, legislation may even be enacted forcing you to collect and submit sales tax to every state from which you've made a sale. Currently, you are only required to do this for sales generated from the state in which your business is located.

There are many tax changes in the works for the future when it comes to online selling. Keep abreast of new laws as they are enacted. At the very least, learn as much as you can about properly reporting your online income and expenses. If you are doing it right, you have little to worry about. This book is an excellent place to start.

Updates

The tax law is ever changing. Dollar limit amounts listed in this book are the most likely to be shifted. Congress is regularly amending the tax code. Dollar limits are generally altered to reflect inflation. Other changes also occur to alter behavior. Some changes are temporary. Some changes are permanent. You can stay up to date with the latest tax laws affecting online sellers by visiting: www.irs.gov. The IRS website is a gold mine of information. They put out Publication 553 each year. This is a booklet highlighting new tax changes. It is also available on the IRS website in PDF form. Updates to information in this book may also be found at:

www.taxesforonlinesellers.com.

Throughout this book, you will find explanations of what to fill in, line by line, on certain tax forms. Please be aware the tax forms may change slightly each year. Line 9 of last year's form may be line 10 next year. Use this book, and the tax forms located in the back, as a reference to compare to current tax forms.

Mistakes

If, after reading this book, you realize you've made a mistake on a past return, you may file an amended return (Form 1040X p.145). You generally have three years from when you filed the original return to file an amendment to it. This form must be mailed. It can not be e-filed.

Note: The years listed in this book refer to the year you are filing taxes for. For instance, if it says (2007), you will be filing taxes by April of 2008 for the year (2007).

Taxes for
Online Sellers

Business Entity
Chapter 1

When you find yourself making money from online selling, you are in business. (See Chapter 14 to make the determination if your business is a hobby.) If you claim business profit on a Schedule C, you are in business. When filing taxes on income from a new business, the IRS does not care if you have a business license. Local statutes will determine whether or not you need one. They generally will only cost around $20, and the paperwork to obtain one is simple. Contact your local Chamber of Commerce to find out more.

If you are the only person who could be considered the owner of your business, you are a sole proprietor and will file a Schedule C along with your 1040. This book is written with the sole proprietor in mind. It is the easiest entity to file. The next two pages contain brief explanations of different business entities, though keep in mind, many of the circumstances in this book have different rules if your business is not a sole proprietorship.

Sole Proprietor

You and your business are one and the same to the IRS. You may have heard of DBA. This means "doing business as." If your username on eBay is Tallskylark, you may decide to use that as your business name. This means you are: Buddy Smith DBA Tallskylark. It is also referred to as filing a fictitious name.

Your business profits (or losses) as a sole proprietor are figured on a Schedule C (p.129), then transferred to your individual tax return (1040) along with personal income. In community property states, both spouses can be considered co-owners of a sole proprietorship. In the other states, however, co-owners are considered a partnership.

Partnership

A partnership is a business of two or more people. The business passes its income or losses on to the individual partners. The partnership, itself, does not pay any taxes (the partners as individuals do), but must file an annual tax return. Limits, such as Section 179 limits (discussed in Chapter 7) are split between the partners in a partnership.

Limited Partnership

A limited partnership is made up of at least one general manager liable for an unlimited amount of business debt, and one or more limited partners whose liability is limited to their investment in the business.

Family Limited Partnership

A family limited partnership is a business that is a limited partnership, made up of only related members. A family limited partnership can be used to pass a business to adult children at a tax savings.

Limited Liability Company

A limited liability company is a form of business taxed much like a partnership. On the other hand, the business, not the individual, is liable for the business debt, as with a corporation.

Corporation

A corporation is a state-registered business owned by shareholders. The business itself files and pays taxes.

S Corporation

An S corporation is a corporation that elects to pass its income or loss through to its shareholders instead of being taxed as a business.

Forms and Publications
Chapter 2

How Tax Laws Work

Congress enacts laws which become the tax code, or Internal Revenue Code (IRC). If you want to view this code in its full form, it can be located at: www4.law.cornell.edu/uscode/26.

Then, the Internal Revenue Service (IRS), part of the Treasury Department, interprets and fills in the code in what are called Treasury Regulations. They further explain how the code should be applied by distributing Publications.

You figure and report income and deductions on tax forms. Generally, each form also has instructions further explaining how to fill in the forms.

If a taxpayer fights the results of an audit, he does so in tax court. A federal judge may sustain or reject the IRS interpretation of the tax code. You may view judgments of tax code interpretations at www.ustaxcourt.gov.

Forms

Listed below are some forms you may need to file as an online seller. I also included some publications, produced by the IRS, which may be of assistance when filling out forms. Don't forget, the IRS also puts out instructions to most forms. This is not an all-encompassing list, nor will you necessarily need to use many of these forms. Read the individual chapters in this book for more information regarding which forms you may need personally.

In Appendix A, you will find a copy of most forms discussed within the book. I wanted to put them all together in one place for easy reference. You should look over each form as you read the information pertaining to that form to have a visual to help you understand everything explained in the individual chapters.

List of Forms

Form 1040—Standard form most everyone needs. The other forms listed, if needed, will be filed along with your 1040.

Schedule A—To deduct interest, taxes, and casualties related to personal or hobby expenses

Schedule C—To reprt business profits and losses

Schedule D—To report capital gains or losses

Schedule SE—To figure and pay self-employment tax on any income from a trade or business

Form SS-4—To apply for an Employer Identification Number

Form W-2—Wage and Tax Statement

Form W-3—Transmittal of Wage and Tax Statements

Form W-4—Employee's Withholding Allowance Certificate

Form 940—Employer's Annual Federal Unemployment

Form 941—Employer's Quarterly Federal Tax Return

Form 944—Employer's Annual Federal Tax Return

Form 1040 ES – U.S. Estimated Tax for Individuals

Form 1040X—Amended U.S. Individual Tax Return

Form 1099-Misc.—Miscellaneous Income

Form 3115—To inform the IRS of a change in accounting method

Form 3621—NOL Carry-Over

Form 4562—To claim depreciation on or to deduct direct costs of certain business property

Form 4684—To report a casualty or theft gain or loss involving business assets.

Form 4797—To report sales, exchanges, or involuntary conversions of business property.

Form 5500EZ—Annual Return of One Participant (Owners and Their Spouses) Retirement Plan

Form 8109B—Federal Deposit Coupon

Form 8494—To report the buying or selling of a business, or of a group of assets which comprise a business

Form 8824 – To report like-kind exchanges (trade-in).

Form 8829—To report the business use of your home

Publications

Publication 15—Circular E—Employer's Tax Guide

Publication 334—Tax guide for small business

Publication 463—Travel, entertainment, gift, and car expenses

Publication 505—Tax withholding and Estimated Tax

Publication 523—Selling your home

Publication 535—Business expenses

Publication 536—Net operating losses

Publication 538—Accounting periods and methods

Publication 538—Inventories

Publication 544—Sales and other disposition of assets

Publication 547—Casualties, disasters, and thefts

Publication 551—Basis of assets

Publication 553—Highlights of tax changes

Publication 560—Retirement plans for small business

Publication 583—Starting a business and keeping records

Publication 587—Business use of your home

Publication 919—Explanations on adjusting the amount withheld from a regular paycheck of you or your spouse

Publication 946—How to depreciate property

Publication 1635—Understanding your EIN (employer identification number).

Publication 1976—Independent contractor or employee

Publication 3328—How to file your child's tax return

All of these forms and publications are available in PDF format from the IRS website—www.irs.gov. Many may also be found at your local library. You can link to the IRS forms from www.taxesforonlinesellers.com.

Keeping Records
Chapter 3

Keep records!! Spend time every week, or at least every month, reconciling your records. Suggestions for ways to keep records are spreadsheets, accounting or small business software, and keeping an accordion style folder with spaces for each category. Print out blank spreadsheets and fill the cells in with pen as you spend. Keep an account book or expense diary/log.

What Records are Necessary?

Necessary information for each purchase includes: date, name of payee, and amount of expense. This information is necessary if you choose to use bank or credit card statements as documentation, as well. Accounting computer software allows you to categorize things as you type them in for easy organization later. At the very least, keep receipts in envelopes, by category and month, and write the total on the outside.

According to IRS Publication 946, you ". . . must maintain an account book, diary, log, statement of expense, trip sheet, or similar record or other documentary evidence that, together with the receipt, is sufficient to establish each element of an expenditure or use . . ."

> **You must have records of:**
>
> - The cost of each item
> - The amount of each use (business vs. personal)
> - The date purchased and used
> - The business purpose

You may write any necessary information not provided on the back of a receipt. In the case of making purchases from individuals where receipts aren't given, such as at a yard sale, keep a log book with all the necessary information. Even have the seller sign what you've written, if possible.

In most circumstances, you will not need to send any of these records to the IRS along with your tax forms. In the case of an audit, however, you will be expected to provide this documentation for review.

Record Keeping Computer Software

I can't emphasize enough how important all of your bookkeeping is. Computer software can be invaluable. Some programs help figure taxes and prepare tax forms. Still others will even help you keep track of your inventory. Some examples are: Quick-Books, Peachtree, Turbo Tax, Quicken, and Tax Cut. Some of the accounting software also integrates with the tax software mentioned.

Bank Deposits

Whether you use a business or personal checking account for business, you need to make a note of every deposit in both accounts. If you are ever audited, you will have to account for every deposit. If you can't prove (through at least your own journaling) the deposit was child support, you may be taxed on it. Keeping a separate checking account for the business will be important later, in Chapter 14. As a sole proprietor, you don't necessarily have to have an account in the business name. Just make sure it is in your name, and is kept separate from your personal finances. It will also make keeping track of income and expenses much easier.

Business vs. Personal Records

For all business equipment, keep records of business vs. personal use. For instance, if you are deducting the cost of a computer, you will need to keep a notebook beside it. Jot down every time you used it, and how you used it (business or personal). This will be important later when determining how much of its purchase price you may deduct.

How Long Should Records be Kept?

Typically, you can be audited for three years after the date you file your return. However, for serious issues, it can extend for six years, and if the IRS feels it is outright fraud, there is no time limit. If you expense business equipment and sell it at a loss, you will have to potentially recapture that loss (explained in Chapter 8) for up to five years. So, my advice is to keep all your records for at least six years. For records pertaining to the purchase of business assets, however, I would keep them until they are no longer likely to apply, or six years after you sell the equipment.

Income
Chapter 4

Any income you (and/or your spouse if filing a joint return) received as wages, tips, salary, or other income reported on a W-2 should be reported on line 7 of your 1040 (p.126). Income generated through self-employment needs to be figured on a Schedule C, and then transferred to your 1040, line 12 (2006).

The focus of this book is your business income. You must file a Schedule C (p. 129) if you made $400 or more in business income in the year for which you're filing. Even if you made less than $400, it may still be to your advantage to file a Schedule C. If you had any losses after deducting business expenses, those (net operating losses) may be used to offset other income generated by you (or your spouse if married filing jointly).

Accounting Methods

The main accounting methods available to use to keep track of your income and expenses are the cash method, the accrual method, or a combination of both (hybrid). If you change your accounting method in later years, you need to file form 3115 to let the IRS know. You do not need to file Form 3115 (p.144) in order to initially choose your accounting method. You will only need it if you change that method in future years.

Cash

Under the cash method, you account for your income in the year in which it is *received*. Businesses with inventories aren't typically allowed to file under the cash method, but there is an exception. If your average annual gross receipts for the business total under $1,000,000.00 (one million) you are allowed to use the cash method. Since the majority of online sellers don't gross a million dollars per year, most of us may use the cash method.

The cash method is the easiest to account for. Simply total your income for the year in which it was received. If money was transferred to your bank account before the year ended, even if it didn't register as in the bank until January, count it for the previous year. You were *paid* in December.

Accrual

Under the accrual method, you count income in the year in which you *earned* it. If you rendered services in November, but weren't paid for them until February, you would count it as November's income. This doesn't make sense to a lot of people, because it is not the way we automatically think about money. Most of us don't need to use the accrual method, but may if we choose to.

Cash and accrual methods of accounting pertain to how you account for both your income and expenses.

Totaling Your Income

How much income did your business generate this past year? This is where we figure the total amount you were paid before deductions. If you accept credit cards through your own site, you'll need to gather all payment statements/receipts. Any time you accept cash, check, or a money order, you should write a receipt. This can be done through a small-business computer program or in a receipt book where you hand write receipts.

If you sell through established sites, chances are you're paid directly through that site, through something like Paypal, or merchant accounts through credit card companies. In all cases, you should be able to print out monthly (or by pay period) statements. Every site differs on how long this information is available, so it is best to get into the habit of printing out and reconciling your records at least monthly. The printer ink it takes to print out all of these records is deductible later on Part II of your Schedule C.

You will not receive a W-2 or 1099 from these sites. Which means that, no, eBay is not reporting your income to the IRS, yet. But, you sold something with the intent of making profit, so you are obligated to report it on your taxes. If you are ever audited, the IRS will pay close attention to deposits made into your bank account. You will have to account for these. During an audit, the IRS may subpoena records from online venues. This also means taxes are not being withheld from your income. You still owe them, but we will get to that in more detail later.

Fees

Some fees for selling online are charged up front. Either you pay a one time fee to list items, or you are charged individual fees for each feature you'd like to appear in your listing, (i.e. bold print). If you are charged these fees up front, keep records of them. Those fees will be deducted separately under your deductions. Do not deduct them from your income just yet.

If, however, fees or commissions are deducted from your proceeds before you get paid, (i.e. Amazon takes 15% of the selling price) then there are two ways to record this on your taxes. You can choose to ignore them in essence, only claiming as income what you actually received as payment. Include any postage/shipping credits you were paid by the customer. In this example, you would simply add the $155 to your income. You were only *paid* $155.

Example: Sales + postage credits	$200.00
Minus Fees	- $45.00
Transferred to checking	$155.00

The other method is to include the $200 as income, and list the $45 under commissions and fees in the deductions category (Line 10, Part II, Schedule C.) It works out the same either way. Whatever you do, stay consistent. Do not accidentally deduct the same fees in both places.

Refunds/Returns

Generally, funds for returned items will be handled through the same source handling your payments.

> **Example:** A customer wants a refund of a book she purchased from Craig through Amazon and then returned to him. He goes to his seller account page, and submits for a refund. The refunded amount will automatically be deducted out of Craig's next deposit from Amazon.

In this case, the refunded amount may be ignored, as with the fees explained earlier. Otherwise, you count it into your original income now, and then deduct it on line 2 of your Schedule C, Returns and allowances.

Bad Debts

If you mail out merchandise to the customer before you get paid, you risk not getting paid at all. Avoid this. If it happens, however, you must attempt to collect the debt by repeated contacts with the customer. If, after a period of time, you still cannot collect the debt, the uncollected part becomes a business bad debt.

You can only claim the amount of the debt you previously included as income. Therefore, if you use the cash method, you never count it as income because you never received it. In this case, you cannot count it as a bad debt.

Do include costs, such as postage, under expenses. Do not include the item in your ending inventory. (Both discussed later.) This way, you lose the profit potential you had, but have recapped all expenses and the original cost you paid for the item.

If you later receive payment for the item, simply add it into your income when received. You will have then already deducted all expenses associated with the item.

Barter and Trade

What if you accept or offer inventory as trade?

> **Example:** Kim hires Richard to install shelving for her inventory storage for $50. While there, Richard notices a couple of CD's in Kim's inventory he'd like to have. They come up with a plan. Richard will install the shelves for $25 cash, plus two CD's. Richard should claim $50 worth of income. He received $25 in cash and $25 worth of barter income.

What is Not Income

Any loans your business received are NOT considered income. If your business has to repay it, it is not counted. Do not include, on line 1 of Schedule C, any amounts received from selling business assets. That will be added later in Chapter 8.

Acceptable Records for Income

If you say you made money, the IRS will pretty much take your word for it. The problem arises when there is a question you may not be reporting *all* your income. Make sure there are no lapses in your recording method. Examples of this would be pages missing from your receipt book (receipts are numbered) or pay periods not printed from your online source.

If you have no sales to show for the month of February, for instance, there will generally be a page showing February (or said pay period) at the top. It may say there are no records to show. Print out that page and include it in your file along with all other pay periods showing income. Chances are you were still charged fees for that month if you had listings but nothing sold. This page may list that. You would want to keep that information for later deductions, anyway.

Summary

Add up all of your income from receipt books, online statement printouts, visa/master card statements, and any other business income you received through sales. This is your gross receipts and sales, reported on line 1 of the Schedule C. Congratulations! In later chapters we'll get that number down with honest deductions to lower your tax obligation.

Inventory
Chapter 5

(Schedule C)

Keeping Records of Purchases

Total every dollar (and penny) used to purchase items for resale. Keep all receipts of purchases made for resale at any store or thrift shop. Make sure you ask for a receipt if you aren't handed one. Some of the thrift type places don't readily hand them out. Keep receipts or packing slips from stores, wholesalers, and publishing companies— basically, ALL RECEIPTS! You may also use credit card statements, bank statements, and even cancelled checks as receipts as long as they show all necessary information. Make sure your receipts show the date, name of payee (store name), and amount of the expense. If it doesn't also detail what you purchased, write that on the back.

Cost of Goods Sold

You'll need to skip to Part III of your Schedule C (p.130) before you can complete part one.

Cost

I've already emphasized keeping track of what you pay for your inventory. A spreadsheet becomes invaluable at this point. List the item you purchased, where you purchased it and the price you paid for it. There are many inventory and accounting computer software programs on the market to help. Keep your receipts as back-up verification. When the item sells, go back to your spreadsheet and mark it as sold.

At the end of the year, add up the total you spent on inventory. (This is your cost of inventory number.) Then, add up the amount spent on just the inventory *not* marked as sold. (This is your ending inventory number.) We'll assume this is the first year you've had inventory, so your beginning inventory equals zero. If you claimed inventory last year, simply use your ending inventory from last year as your beginning inventory this year.

$0.00	beginning inventory
+ $3589.00	cost of inventory purchased
-$1692.00	ending inventory
= $1897.00	cost of goods sold

On Part III of Schedule C, add your beginning inventory to your purchases. Then, subtract your ending inventory. The result is your cost of goods sold.

Yes, this means you don't get to claim a deduction of the purchase price of inventory until it sells.

Fair Market Value

There are two main methods of calculating the value of your ending inventory. The above example illustrates the cost method. The other option is the lower of cost or fair market value method. This will usually be cost for most of us. This means your inventory, for tax purposes, is worth what you paid for it.

The only times it might make sense, for an online seller of used goods, to use the fair market value method is if your inventory declines in value and is no longer worth even what you paid for it, or when selling personal items you already owned (discussed later).

Hiring a professional to appraise your inventory will tell you if you should claim cost or fair market value if you are in question, though the cost of an appraiser will probably offset any savings you may otherwise realize.

Materials and Supplies

In part three of the Schedule C, Cost of Goods Sold (p.130), there are spaces to account for materials, supplies, labor, and other costs. These headings are generally referring to other money you spent to either make something to sell or improve something in order to sell it.

These categories are supposed to be handled in the same way as inventory, in that, they shouldn't be deducted specifically until the item they are used for has sold. Do not pay yourself labor. This line is intended to be used to account for fees paid to others for labor done to improve, repair, or manufacture your inventory.

If You Make Your Own Inventory

If you are a crafter, woodworker, artist, or create your own inventory in any other common form, you do not specifically have to account for inventory. You list all of the supplies, which become a part of your finished inventory, under materials and supplies. Once again, do not pay yourself labor. You may list these materials and supplies here, and deduct them, once your item sells. You may prorate the cost of the amount of each supply used if all of your items do not sell in a given tax year.

> **Example:** Alan is an artist. He purchases several tubes of paint at $5 each, but no one painting uses more than a tube of paint, and he used just a little of each color. At the end of the year, he has only sold two paintings he used the purchased paint to create.
>
> Alan may prorate the dollar amount he believes equals the quantity of paint consumed for the two paintings he sold. He may not deduct the rest of the cost of the paint until more paintings sell.

Special Provision for Qualifying Taxpayers

There is a provision, which allows certain small business taxpayers to not account for inventories. This means you may deduct your inventory costs as you would other materials and supplies. However, you are not allowed to deduct the cost until the item has sold.

Auditors are specifically on the lookout for online sellers who deduct the cost of inventory before it has sold. It is to your benefit, in the case of an audit, to figure the cost of your goods sold as described in this chapter. The same amount of record keeping and paperwork is necessary either way.

Consignments

Do not include items, consigned to you to sell, as inventory in your possession. One way you can account for it once you do sell it, however, is to count the amount you paid to the item's original owner as the cost you paid for the item. In this circumstance, you count it in your purchased and sold inventories only after it sells.

> **Example:** Rob gave Jennifer a stereo to sell online for him in November 2006. It did not sell that year. On Jennifer's 2006 return, the stereo does not exist.
>
> The stereo sold in January 2007 for $75. The agreement was for Jennifer to pay Rob 2/3 of the selling price and keep 1/3 for herself.
>
> On Jennifer's 2007 return, she'll include $50 under line 36, Schedule C, purchases—the amount she paid Rob for the stereo. She will include $75 under income on line 1.
>
> It is as if she purchased the stereo from Rob for $50, and sold it for $75, making a $25 profit.

Inventory Never Received

What if you pay in advance for a shipment of inventory from a wholesaler, and you never receive your items? I am referring to a situation in which there is little chance of you ever receiving what you paid for. For instance, possibly the wholesaler has gone out of business.

You list the amount paid under cost of inventory. Do not include it in your ending inventory, because it doesn't exist. This way, you are deducting the amount you paid from your income. In essence, you are getting your money back.

If, in the future, you receive the inventory, you will then count it in that future year's ending inventory (if it hasn't yet sold). You will have already deducted the purchase price.

Personal Items Converted to Inventory

When you began selling online, you probably started by selling off some of the personal items you no longer needed. When figuring your cost of goods sold, do not neglect to give these items value. Unless you still have the receipt from where you purchased them, however, you will have to value these items by "fair market value." This is simple enough to do with these items. If you have already sold the item, the fair market value is what you sold it for. If you have not sold the item yet, simply research similar items on a site like eBay. Average the prices the similar items are going for to come up with the fair market value for your item.

In order to keep accurate records of how you came up with your value in the case of an audit, it is advisable to print out a few pages showing similar items being sold at the same price at which you valued your item.

Inventory Disposal

If you end up with worthless inventory you are no longer able to sell, you may dispose of it, reducing the value of that particular part of your inventory. You need to document the disposal by photo, video, receipts, or a statement by a reputable third party. If you sell it at a loss, even to a resale shop, count the amount you received as income and track it as a sale in all ways. In that case, it does not apply as inventory disposal.

For more information about inventories, see IRS Publication 538.

Expenses
Chapter 6

(Schedule C)

Ordinary and Necessary

You may generally deduct those business expenses that are ordinary and necessary expenses of a trade or business and incurred during the tax year. Ordinary is defined as one that is common and accepted in a particular business activity. Necessary is defined as an expense that is appropriate and helpful to the business.

Schedule C, Part II (p.129)

Advertising, line 8

If you pay for a website from which you sell your products, you may deduct the cost under advertising. Do you have business cards? Do you have bookmarks with your business name printed on them? Those are all included here. If, however, you made your own business cards or bookmarks, you would deduct the cost of the paper stock and computer ink under office expenses. Anything used to promote your business is generally advertising.

Car and Truck Expenses, line 9

You may list most of your automobile expenses here, unless you need to file Form 4562 for depreciation. Automobile expenses are discussed in Chapter 9.

Commissions and Fees, line 10

Here's where you will deduct any fees or commissions incurred from your online selling venues. Do you pay for an online look-up service (Scout Pal)? Do you pay monthly or yearly fees to an online postage company, separate from the postage you claimed under office expenses? Do you pay for Amazon Pro Merchant status or an eBay store? Don't forget entrance fees into that big sale. Do you have a separate bank account for the business, for which you are charged service fees? Any fees or commissions, not otherwise ignored while figuring income (as discussed in Chapter 4), are deductible here.

Contract Labor, line 11

Contract labor not deductible on lines 17, 21, 26, or 37.

Depreciation and Section 179 Deductions, line 13

Line 13 is where you'll list any depreciation or Section 179 deductions you figure on Form 4562. This is discussed in the next chapter.

Insurance, line 15

Did you buy separate insurance to protect your inventory? Any insurance premiums you pay (non-medical), directly related to the business, are deductible here. Do not add this amount here and under insurance on Form 8829, if you expense your home office.

Heath Insurance—While we are on the subject of insurance, I'll give you a brief run-down of another tax break you may take. If you are self-employed, and provide health insurance coverage to yourself and/or family, you may generally deduct 100% of your premiums to arrive at your AGI on line 29 of your 1040.

This is providing you pay for the premiums with income generated from your business. You also may not have a subsidized health plan available to you through your employer or the employer of your spouse. Use the worksheet in the 1040 instructions to help you figure the amount.

Interest, line 16a/16b

16a – Mortgage interest you paid, on real property (building/house/warehouse) associated with your business, other than your main home, for which you received a Form 1098. If you secured a loan for business property with your home, the interest could be deductible. Check Publication 535 (Business Expenses) for more information.

16b – Here is where you can deduct interest on loans or credit card debts that are specifically related to business purchases.

Legal and Professional Services, line 17

You may deduct the cost of tax advice and preparation directly related to the business. Ask your tax preparer what portion of their fee applied to the business only.

Office Expenses, line 18

Here's where you will list all of your office expenses. Think of this as including everything consumable you can do from your desk. Things like ink pens, printer ink, paper, and even postage. If it gets used up at your desk and needs replacing, total that expense here. Generally, most of these items will have store receipts. Simply total the receipts. Postage, however, may be a little trickier.

Postage

If you sell anything online, chances are you visit your post office frequently, if not daily. If you allow the teller to weigh and stamp your packages, you will receive a receipt at the end of the transaction. Keep these and add them together for your postage total. Yes, even delivery confirmation is deductible.

If, however, you print your own postage online, you won't have an envelope of receipts. Just like totaling your income, there are ways of extracting this information using your computer. Either by visiting the website of the company you use for postage, or through their software stored on your computer, you will be able to print out statements of how much postage you've purchased through them and when it was used. Print these pages for your records. Print these pages out regularly because you never know how long they will be available.

Pension and Profit Sharing Plans, line 19

Deduction for contributions to a pension, profit sharing, or annuity plan. For the self-employed only in the plan themselves, this number comes from Form 5500EZ. Do not include amounts you paid on your own behalf as an employee of your own company. That amount will go on line 28 of your 1040.

Self-Employment Retirement Plans

An additional note on retirement plans for the self-employed. Everyone can deduct a certain amount of his or her retirement contributions on their personal tax return. Self-employed individuals may also be able to deduct set-up costs and additional amounts from their self-employment income. It is very beneficial to read through IRS Publication 560 (Retirement Plans for Small Business). It not only explains deductions you may take and where to take them, but also helps you determine which type of qualifying plan is right for you.

Rent or Lease, line 20a/20b

20a – Here is where you list the amount you paid to rent or lease machinery or equipment. Don't forget to only list the business percentage of the rent if you don't use the item 100% for business. (Business time used ÷ total time used = business percentage—your answer will be a decimal number. Multiply that decimal by 100 to find your business percent.) (Total amount paid x business % = amount you may deduct.) Check Publication 463 for more information on leased *vehicles*.

20b – You may deduct your rent or lease payments for offsite storage or warehousing space for your inventory. Any office equipment you rent or lease may also be expensed here.

Repairs and Maintenance, line 21

Costs of maintaining or repairing business equipment are deductible. The cost to improve something (like adding more memory to your computer) is able to be depreciated over time, but is not deductible on this line. (See page 59 for more information on repairing vs. improving.) Do not include any expense you are deducting on another form, such as Business Use of the Home (8829).

Supplies, line 22

Here is where you get to claim your packaging materials. Any cost for boxes, envelopes, b-flute, bubble wrap, tape, or other packaging supplies may be written off under supplies.

Taxes and Licenses, line 23

The business percentage of your state and local personal property taxes, payable on your business assets, go here. This includes the business percentage of vehicle personal property taxes regardless of whether you used the standard mileage rate or actual expenses (Chapter 9). You may claim the fee you pay to obtain a business license. You may also claim the half of Social Security and Medicare, and all of the unemployment the business paid for employees (Chapter 11).

Travel, line 24a/24b

Besides mileage (line 9), you may also claim other business travel expenses. Usually, you may claim the reasonable cost of a hotel room, if you are far enough away from home to justify needing rest, and 50% of your meals.

The IRS considers qualifying business travel expenses to include any ordinary and necessary expenses incurred by a taxpayer while away from home in the conduct of trade or business. These include travel, meals, transportation, a reasonable amount for baggage, hotel rooms, telephone and fax services, and costs of maintaining a car for business purposes.

If you go to an antique book convention on the beach and you primarily deal in antique books, it would be deductible. However, if you go to the beach and check out a few antique stores looking for books while there, the IRS may question how necessary that travel was.

What if your family tags along? You are only allowed to deduct the same expenses as if you traveled alone. Unless, of course, you have hired your family members as employees (Chapter 11), and then you can deduct their expenses as you can your own.

See IRS Publication 463 for more information.

Utilities, line 25

You may deduct utilities used for your business. A separate phone line, for business only, is deductible here. Do not include this amount here and under utilities if you file form 8829 for home office expenses. This line is for utilities used 100% for business, such as electricity in a rented warehouse.

Wages, line 26

Salaries and wages paid to employees and independent contractors. Do not deduct amounts paid to yourself or those deducted elsewhere on your return.

Other Expenses

On Part V (5) of your Schedule C, the IRS gives you room to list other expenses not clearly identifiable on Part II. Examples of other expenses you may incur are listed below. Your total from these, line 48, will be carried over to line 27 of Part II of your Schedule C.

Education

You may deduct education expenses if the education is to maintain or improve a skill required by your current business or trade. Tuition, fees, books, course supplies, etc. You may not deduct education expenses related to get rich quick or financial seminars, or if they qualify you for a new trade or business. eBay University seminars are deductible if you are already in the business.

Internet Service

You may deduct the business portion of internet service. Make certain to keep detailed records of when it was used, and whether it was business or personal use. Figure your business percentage based on these records. (Business time ÷ total time = business percentage)

Business Publications and Books

You may deduct any book or other publication used in learning how to better run your business. This even includes the book you have in your hand. Magazines and newsletters geared toward a topic related to your business count, as well.

Line 28 – Total expenses

Here you will total all of the expenses you have taken in Part II of your Schedule C.

For more information on qualifying business expenses, see IRS Publication 535.

Equipment Deductions and Depreciation
Chapter 7

(Form 4562)

Words you need to understand before reading this chapter:

Basis—Typically, the cost of an item. This amount may be increased by sales tax and improvements.

Business Basis—Multiply the basis of your item by the percentage you use the item for business purposes. The result is your business basis in the item.

Improvements vs. Repairs—Imagine a number line. The condition of an item when you purchased it is in the center of your number line, at zero. Wear and tear, including damages, drag the condition number down into the negatives. When you *repair* something, you are simply getting it back to zero, the original condition, on your number line. When you *improve* something, you are improving the condition into the positive numbers on your number line. You are making the item better than it was when you purchased it.

In the last chapter, Expenses, you may have wondered where the line to deduct the amount you spent on equipment purchased for your business was. Equipment is considered a business asset. (The terms equipment, item, property, and asset are used interchangeably in this chapter.) It is expected to have a life of longer than one year, wearing out over time. Therefore, the IRS expects you to depreciate the cost over a specified number of years (class life or classification) depending on the item. Depreciation simply means deducting a certain percentage of the cost of the item per year, until you have fully deducted your business investment in it.

A list of items that might be common to online selling, and their classifications are:

3 years—off the shelf computer software
5 years—cars, trucks, trailers, computers and peripherals, copiers, calculators.
7 years—office furniture, fixtures, personal property that does not fit into other categories (see IRS publication 946 for more detailed lists.)

Section 179

If, however, you meet the following criteria, you may simply deduct the full cost of the item in the year purchased instead of depreciating (spreading it out little by little over a number of years). Except for automobiles, which have their own rules, you can deduct most equipment expenses in the year you purchase and put it to use in your business under Internal Revenue Code, Section 179.

In order to use Section 179:

● You must have taxable income of at least the amount you expense. This taxable income can come from the business, another business claimed by you, other wages and tips, and even your spouse's wages and tips if married filing jointly.

● You can either expense (Section 179) or depreciate, not both, on the same item in the same year. Though there are special rules that enable you to depreciate the remaining amount of an item in future years you weren't able to fully expense this year. If your income doesn't support the Section 179 deduction, you may want to consider using regular depreciation rules, instead.

● You have to use the item more than 50% for business purposes. If you use it less than 100% for business, you can only claim the percentage of the purchase price based on the percentage used in business. If your usage drops below 50%, (explained in Chapter 8) you may have to pay recapture taxes. If you *start out* using it less than 50% for business, you will have to depreciate it instead of using Section 179.

● You should still use that equipment 50% or more for business purposes over the number of years you would have otherwise depreciated it (i.e. computer used 5 years).

● You may not use Section 179 if you purchased the item from a relative.

Limits Section 179

The current total dollar amount allowed in Section 179 deductions is $125,000 (2007). (The example form in the back of the book still quotes amounts from 2006.) That number is expected to go down to $25,000 by 2010; however, there are current proposals to keep it higher. Section 179 deductions are reported on form 4562 (Depreciation and Amortization). If your income does not support deducting the full amount of deductions you have, you can carry forward your deductions to the following year, assuming you have taxable income equal to or greater than your current and carry-over deductions in that following year. Or, you may elect to depreciate the remaining amount in years to come.

> **Section 179 does NOT apply to:**
> - Real estate
> - Inventory
> - Gifts or inheritance
> - Property purchased from a relative
> - Items you already owned in a previous year and are converting to business use
> - Heating and air conditioner units

Listed Property Section 179

Section 179 has provisions for certain assets the IRS considers having the potential for personal use. These items are called "listed property." Computers, vehicles, and cell phones fall into this category. For these items you must keep detailed records of business versus personal use. Just keep a notebook next to the computer, for instance. Whenever the item is in use, jot down when and for how long, and whether it was business or personal. This may sound tedious, but during an audit, you will have to produce this notebook.

Depreciation

Depreciation is a deduction allowed to offset the normal wear and tear of business equipment. You may not depreciate an item used solely for personal purposes.

The Modified Accelerated Cost Recovery System (MACRS) is the system of depreciation currently in place. It applies to most business property placed in service after 1986.

> **MACRS property is depreciable if it is tangible personal property which:**
>
> - Wears out,
> - Has a useful life exceeding one year, AND
> - Is used in your business.

Under MACRS, there are different methods and conventions for depreciating your items. You will have to use both one method and one convention when depreciating an item.

Methods:

Declining Balance
The General Depreciating System (GDS) is the standard, accelerated method of depreciation under MACRS. Using the GDS 200% declining balance (200DB) method (150% for 15 and 20 year property) means you get to deduct more of the item's value in the early years of its recovery period.

Straight Line
The straight-line (S/L) method of depreciation allows you to deduct the value of your item equally over the recovery period.

Alternative Depreciation

The Alternative Depreciation System (ADS) uses the straight-line method of depreciation over a specified number of years. The recovery period for ADS is usually a little longer than used under general or straight-line depreciation methods. (Figure 7:1)

Figure 7:1 Comparison of GDS vs. ADS Recovery Periods

	GDS	ADS
Passenger automobile	5 years	5 years
Computers/Peripherals	5 years	5 years
Office furniture & equip.	7 years	10 years
Heavy trucks, trailers	5 years	6 years
Calculator, copier, etc.	5 years	7 years
Personal property with no class life assigned	7 years	12 years

A complete list may be found in Appendix B of Publication 946.

Conventions:

Half-Year

Under the half-year convention, your item is treated as though it was purchased and placed in service at the mid-point of the tax year it was purchased, no matter when during the year the purchase was actually made. Therefore, only half of the otherwise allowable depreciation amount is able to be deducted during the first year.

The half-year convention is standard with all depreciation and must be used unless the mid-quarter convention rules apply. (Except in the case of depreciating the business use of your home, in which case the mid-month convention applies the first year. This is explained in Chapter 10.) The half-year convention is built into the tables shown in Figures 7:2–7:3.

> **Example:** Using the straight-line method (because it's easier for me to demonstrate the half-year example using S/L), Morgan is able to depreciate her office desk, used 100% for business, over a seven year recovery period. Her basis in it (the amount she paid) is $700. She is able to take equal, $100 deductions each of the seven years. Because of the half-year convention, however, she may only deduct half of that in the first year.
>
> | | |
> |---|---|
> | Year one -$50 | Year five -$100 |
> | Year two -$100 | Year six -$100 |
> | Year three - $100 | Year seven - $100 |
> | Year four -$100 | Year eight -$50 |
>
> Morgan may continue to take a deduction into an additional year (year eight) beyond the desk's recovery period (seven years) in order to fully depreciate it.

Mid-Quarter Convention

Under the mid-quarter convention, all property placed in service during a particular quarter of the year is treated as having been acquired at the mid-point of that quarter. Tables with the mid-quarter convention built in may be found in Publication 946.

The mid-quarter convention only applies if more than 40% of the combined bases of property is placed in service during the last three months of the tax year. Section 179 deductions are not included when figuring this amount.

You can avoid the mid-quarter convention in a couple of ways. Plan your purchases, so over 40% of the cost of them doesn't get spent at the end of the year, by buying early or waiting until January. You could also choose to use Section 179 to expense some of your end of the year equipment purchases. Those items' bases would then not be a part of your calculation of the 40% mark.

Figuring Your Basis

In order to use the tables shown in Figures 7:2–7:3, you first need to figure your item's basis. This is generally the amount you paid for the item, plus any sales tax. Then, you figure your business basis for the item. This is the amount of the item's basis, multiplied by the business percentage of usage. Last, subtract any Section 179 deduction or other credit ever taken on the item.

> **Example:** Elizabeth paid $600 for a laptop computer she uses 70% of the time for business and the rest of the time for personal purposes. She multiplies the laptop's $600 basis by (600 x .70 = $420) 70% to find the amount she may depreciate. If she had taken any previous Section 179 deduction or other credit on the laptop, she would then subtract that amount.

Depreciation Tables

GDS depreciation table including 3, 5, 7, 10, and 15 year property using 200% and 150% Declining Balance with the Half-Year convention built in:

Year	3 Year	5 Year	7 Year	10 Year	15 Year	20 Year
1	33.33%	20%	14.29%	10%	5%	3.750%
2	44.45	32	24.49	18	9.50	7.219
3	14.81	19.20	17.49	14.40	8.55	6.677
4	7.41	11.52	12.49	11.52	7.70	6.177
5		11.52	8.93	9.22	6.93	5.713
6		5.76	8.92	7.37	6.23	5.285
7			8.93	6.55	5.90	4.888
8			4.46	6.55	5.90	4.522
9				6.56	5.91	4.462
10				6.55	5.90	4.461
11				3.28	5.91	4.462
12					5.90	4.461
13					5.91	4.462
14					5.90	4.461
15					5.91	4.462
16					2.95	4.461
17						4.462
18						4.461
19						4.462
20						4.461
21						2.231

(Figure 7:2)

Straight-Line depreciation table through 15 years, with the Half-Year convention built in:

(Use this table under the appropriate number of years to also figure ADS depreciation.)

Year	3 Year	5 Year	7 Year	10 Year	12 Year	15 Year
1	16.67%	10%	7.14%	5%	4.17%	3.33%
2	33.33	20	14.29	10	8.33	6.67
3	33.33	20	14.29	10	8.33	6.67
4	16.67	20	14.28	10	8.33	6.67
5		20	14.29	10	8.33	6.67
6		10	14.28	10	8.33	16.67
7			14.29	10	8.34	6.67
8			7.14	10	8.33	6.66
9				10	8.34	6.67
10				10	8.33	6.66
11				5	8.34	6.67
12					8.33	6.66
13					4.17	6.67
14						6.66
15						6.67
16						3.33

(Figure 7:3)

Figuring Depreciation Using Tables

Once you have the amount you are allowed to depreciate, you multiply the number by that year's percentage from the appropriate depreciation table and column by year.

Continued Example from page 66: Elizabeth's laptop has a recovery period of 5 years. She may depreciate $420 over a five year period. (A total of six years due to the half-year convention.) Using the table in Figure 7:2, Accelerated Depreciation 200DB (also located in Publication 946), Elizabeth finds she can depreciate the following amounts for her laptop (rounded to the nearest dollar):

Business Basis: $420

Year one	$84 (420 x 20%)
Year two	$134 (420 x 32%)
Year three	$81 (420 x 19.20%)
Year four	$48 (420 x 11.52%)
Year five	$48 (420 x 11.52%)
Year six	$24 (420 x 5.76%)

Listed Property

In order to use an accelerated method of depreciation for listed property (automobiles, computers, cell phones, etc.) you must use the equipment more than 50% for business purposes. Remember, listed property consists of those items the IRS considers having the potential for personal use. You must keep records of personal vs. business use for these items. If you use it 50% or less for business purposes, listed property must be depreciated using the Alternative Depreciation System. (Figures 7:1 and 7:3)

If you initially use your listed property over 50% for business, but then it drops in a later year, previous accelerated depreciation deductions are subject to recapture. The amount recaptured is the amount previous deductions exceed the depreciation that would have been allowable under ADS. (See Chapter 8 for more information on recapture.)

Choosing a Depreciation Method

The year you purchase and put your item into use in the business is generally the first year you will take depreciation deductions. That first year is when you will choose what method of depreciation to use. It is standard to use the GDS 200% declining balance method for computing most of your business property. Sometimes, however, you are required to use a different method (usually when business usage is 50% or less on listed property).

You may generally elect to use either the ADS or Straight-Line method for any business property, instead of an accelerated method. The catch to doing so is you must make that election for all property of the same class life put into use in the same year.

> **Example:** If Morgan made the election to depreciate her office desk (7 year property) using the straight-line method, she would also have to use the straight-line method for all other 7-year property purchased and put into use in the same year.

Once you choose a depreciation method, you need to stick with it for that particular item until it is fully depreciated (unless you are required to change, as with business usage dropping to 50% or less).

Converting Personal Equipment to Business

If you purchase equipment for 100% personal use, you may not depreciate it. However, you may begin to depreciate it if and when you decide to begin using it in the business. Your basis for the item is the lesser of the fair market value on the date you placed the item in the business or the original cost of the item, increased by any permanent improvements you have made to it and decreased by any casualty or theft losses ever claimed on it.

Example: Evelyn purchased a PDA for personal planning two years ago. She was no longer using it. It dawned on her she could use it for multiple purposes in her business. She decided to convert it to business property instead of personal property.

Evelyn figured her basis by checking the current fair market value of similar PDA's. She noticed her PDA was no longer going for the amount she paid for it originally. The price on these items had dropped significantly. She averaged the current fair market values she found for similar PDA's. This became her new basis on the item for depreciation purposes.

Filling out the Form (4562) (p.145-146)

Part I, Section 179 Property

Line 1—$125,000(2007) (Section 179 limit)

Line 2—List here the total of all the Section 179 property bases (generally the amount you paid for the items, plus sales tax) combined. If you don't use the item 100% for business, you must write only the business percentage (total cost x business percentage).

Line 3—Threshold amount $500,000 (2007). (This number is expected to go down to $200,000 for years 2010 and after.) Basically, if you list enough Section 179 property above this threshold, your actual limit of $125,000 is reduced, dollar for dollar, by the amount you went over $500,000. Avoid this by keeping your Section 179 deductions under the threshold each year.

Line 4—This line is where you will reduce your $125,000 limit if you went over the threshold. We will assume you didn't for figuring purposes in this book.

Line 5—If you did not go over the threshold of $500,000, you will write $125,000 on this line. It is, once again, your Section 179 limit for this year. (2007) Remember, you will also be limited by your income, line 11.

Line 6 (a)—List the property, individually, which you are expensing under Section 179 (except for listed property).

      6(b)—List your business percentage of the cost of each item (cost x % used for business).

      6(c)—List the amount of that business percentage you are choosing to deduct under Section 179. (This can be the full amount from line 6(b) if your taxable income supports it and you are not over your Section 179 limit.)

Skip to Line 26 (a)—List any *listed property* individually here (used over 50% only).

(b)—Date placed in service

(c)—Percent of business use (i.e. 60%)

(d)—Total cost of purchase

(e)—Business basis (total cost x business percentage)

(f)—Recovery period (i.e. computer—five years)

(g)—Leave blank for Section 179

(h)—Leave blank for Section 179

(i)—The amount you plan to deduct under Section 179. This can be the full amount from line 26(e) if your taxable income supports it and you are not over your Section 179 limit.

Line 29—Add the amounts from line 26(i). List the total here and again on line 7.

Back to Line 7—Enter the amount from line 29. This is the total amount of *listed property* you want to deduct using Section 179.

Line 8—Add the amounts from line 6(c) and line 7. This is the *total* amount you want to deduct using Section 179.

Line 9—List the smaller of the amount you want to deduct or your limit of $125,000.

Line 10—List here any amount you could not deduct last year because you were over your Section 179 limit (or you were over your income limit). (Line 13 of last year's 4562)

Line 11—Enter the smaller of line 5 (your yearly limit) or your total taxable income from any trade or business, including wages or tips earned by you (and/or your spouse if married filing jointly) without regard to any deductions or net operating losses. (For sole-proprietors only)

Line 12—Add your deductions from line 9 to any carry-over from line 10, but do not exceed your limit from line 11.

Line 13—List any amount from line 9 and 10 combined you could not list on line 12 because it was over your income limit. You may carry this amount forward to line 10 of next year's Form 4562.

Skip to Line 22—If you do not have any depreciation deductions to add, simply carry the number from line 12 to here. (If you are also taking depreciation deductions, figure that amount first.) Also then enter this number on line 13, Schedule C.

Filling out the Form (4562) (p. 145-146)

Depreciation

Line 17—You would total here any amount of MACRS depreciation you were taking this year if you had any property for which this is not the first year you were depreciating it.

Line 19—List each item, on the appropriate class year line, that you wish to depreciate, other than listed property.

    (column c)—List your business basis of the cost of each item here, minus any Section 179 deductions or special credits you have previously taken on the item.

    (column d)—List the recovery period here. (i.e. five years for computer)

    (column e)—Enter the convention which applies here. (i.e. HY for half-year or MQ for mid-quarter)

    (column f)—Enter the method of depreciation you are using for each item. (i.e. 200DB, 150DB, or S/L)

    (column g)—Use the tables found in Publication 946 or Form 4562 instructions to figure your allowable depreciation (examples on pages 67-68).

Line 20—You will do the same thing for line 20 as you did for line 19 if you have any property (other than listed property) for which you are using the Alternative Depreciation System (ADS).

Skip to Line 26—Fill in any listed property in columns a-h (described under Section 179, Filling Out the Form, pages 72 and 73) for any listed property on which you want to take depreciation deductions for items used *more* than 50% in your business.

Line 27—Do the same as line 26 for any listed property, used 50% *or less* in your business, on which you want to take depreciation deductions.

Line 28—Add column (h) for both lines 26 and 27. Enter that number here and on line 21.

Back to Line 21—Enter the amount from line 28. This is the total amount of *listed property* you are deducting through depreciation this year.

Line 22—Total line 12 (Section 179 deductions), line 17 (any remaining depreciation from items placed in service in previous years), line 19 (general depreciation which includes straight-line), line 20 (ADS), and line 21 (listed property). Enter the total here and on line 13, Schedule C.

Line 23—Generally will not apply to you. If in doubt, see Regulations section 1.263A-1 IRS.

Additional Notes:

Before taking any Section 179 or depreciation deductions associated with your vehicle or home office, read chapters 9 and 10.

See IRS Publication 946 for more information on everything found in this chapter.

Disposing of Business Equipment
Chapter 8

(Form 4797)

Equipment used in your business is referred to as an asset. (The words equipment, item, property, and asset are used interchangeably in this chapter to refer to the same thing.) There are a few ways and reasons to dispose of business equipment. Mentioned in this book are casualty and theft, like-kind exchanges, sales, and abandonment.

Selling Equipment

The most common way to dispose of equipment used in your business is by selling it. When you sell that asset, however, you will create income from the proceeds you realized on the sale.

If you have taken any Section 179 deductions or depreciation on the equipment, you may be subject to what is called a recapture tax. Don't let this scare you. It is not as bad as it sounds. It simply means a portion of the income you receive from the sale may be taxed as ordinary income, which you might have assumed anyway. Let's see how it works.

Figuring Tax Basis

First we need to figure your tax basis (adjusted basis) in the item. This can be different than your basis or business basis. You figure this by subtracting any Section 179 deductions or other depreciation you've taken on that item over the years, from your investment in it. (Your investment is usually what you paid for it when you purchased it.)

Example: Carol paid $2100 for a business computer. Over the years, she has taken $1737 in accelerated depreciation on it. Her tax basis is now $363.

  $2100.00 original cost basis
 -$1737.00 depreciation taken
 = $363.00 tax basis

If Carol had taken a Section 179 deduction of the entire amount, her tax basis would be $0.

 $2100.00 original cost basis
-$2100.00 section 179 deduction taken
 = $0 tax basis

If Carol had not taken any deductions at all on the item, she would figure her tax basis by subtracting the amount she *could have* depreciated the item if she used straight-line depreciation.

  $2100.00 original cost basis
 -$1470.00 amount she *could have* taken
 = $630.00 tax basis

If you never took any Section 179 deductions or depreciation on the asset, you figure your tax basis using the amount of depreciation that *would have* been allowable had you depreciated it using the straight-line method. Consider the number of years and the amount you could have taken based on the year you purchased and put the asset into use in the business. (You might as well claim it as you're able, since you have to recapture, anyway.)

Form 4797

You report losses and gains of sales of equipment, held longer than one year, on part three of Form 4797 (p. 149-150). Any equipment I can imagine an online seller using (i.e. computer, PDA, shelving, desk, cell phone, heat sealer, etc.) is considered Section 1231 and Section 1245 property. See the Internal Revenue Code, Sections 1231 and 1245 for further descriptions.

> **Section 1231 Property (Only the part of the definition generally affecting online sellers is included here)**—Sales or exchanges of real property or depreciable personal property. This property must be used in a trade or business and held longer than one year . . . (IRS Publication 544)
>
> **Section 1245 Property (Only the part of the definition generally affecting online sellers is included here.)**—Includes any property that is or has been given an allowance for depreciation or amortization and is personal property . . . (IRS Publication 544)

Filling out the Form

On Form 4797, Part III, line 19, you need to list the asset you are selling, the date acquired, and the date sold.

Line 20—You will list the amount of money you received from selling the asset.

Line 20 tells you to see line 1, first. Line 1 references sales or exchanges of real-estate, securities, or commodities reported to you on Form 1099-S or 1099-B, that you are including on this Form 4797. Usually this will not apply to you, but may if you sell your home and claimed business use of it. (Chapter 10)

Line 21—List the amount you originally paid for the item, plus any sales tax paid.

Line 22—List any depreciation, including Section 179 deductions you have taken on the item. As stated earlier, if you have not taken any previous deductions on the asset, include the amount you *could have* depreciated it using straight-line depreciation.

Line 23—This is where you figure your tax basis (adjusted basis). You will subtract the depreciation from your purchase price.

Line 24—Total gain. This is where you will figure your gain or loss by subtracting your adjusted basis from the money you received from selling the asset.

You need to continue filling out lines 25a and 25b, because your asset will generally be considered section 1245 property, as defined earlier. Then, skip to lines 30-32. Generally speaking, you won't have any Section 1250, 1252, 1254, or 1255 property to claim as an online seller. Check those sections under the Internal Revenue Code for descriptions if in doubt. Enter the amount from line 32, other than any part of it from casualty and theft (explained later) on line 6 of the same form.

Depreciation Recapture

Any amount of profit produced from selling an asset, above your tax basis, up to the amount you were allowed to depreciate, is taxed at ordinary income tax rates. Any amount over that is taxed at long-term capital gains rates, unless you have Section 1231 losses from previous years to recapture.

Section 1231 Recapture

Now we need to discuss Section 1231 property. Your business assets from online selling will also generally fall under Section 1231. The way it works is, any Section 1231 gains you receive from selling an asset must be used to offset any Section 1231 losses you've taken any time in this or the past five years. (Yet another reason to keep your records longer than the standard three years.)

> **Example:** In 2004, Sarah sold her heat sealer used for packaging at a loss of $50. In 2005, she sold some old bookshelves, used for inventory storage, at a loss of $25. In 2006, she sold her thermal postage label printer at a gain of $100.
>
> **Result:** On line 6 of Form 4797, she will list her gain on the thermal printer from part three of the same form. On line 7, she will list her gain, but *not* carry it over to Schedule D (pages 131-132) as long-term capital gains. Instead, she will continue to line 8. On line 8, she'll list $75—the amount she claimed as Section 1231 losses in the past five years. Line 9 will direct her to subtract the $75 from her $100 gain from her current year. The remaining $25 will be transferred to Schedule D as a long-term capital gain. Then, the $75 will be carried to line 12. She will figure it through line 18b, and ultimately carry the $75 to line 14 of her 1040, claiming it as ordinary income to offset the prior 1231 losses taken.

Whew! Are you confused yet? Basically, any losses you claimed from the sale of Section 1231 property in the past five years are recaptured as ordinary income, which is generally taxed at a higher rate than long-term capital gains. Any amount over the loss amount you recapture is taxed at the more favorable capital gains rate.

If Sarah had more, previous Section 1231 losses than she could account for in gains this year, all of her gain would be taxed as ordinary income.

> **Example:** Now let's say Sarah has taken losses of $160 over the past few years. Her entire gain for 2006 of $100 was taxed as ordinary income to recapture part of those previous Section 1231 losses. In 2007, she sold her computer for a gain of $200. She will need to claim the outstanding $60 (160 - 100 = 60) of previous Section 1231 losses as ordinary income. The remaining $140 (200 – 60 = 140) will then be taxed as long-term capital gains.

Losses are carried over to your 1040 from line 18b of Form 4797 in the year the item is sold at a loss. Generally, as long as you sell your asset at a price equal to its tax basis, there is no loss or gain.

Most people would assume the sale of their equipment would be taxed as ordinary income, anyway. So, think of all of this as a way you can have a portion of your gain taxed at the more favorable long-term capital gains rate.

Items owned less than one year

If you have had the item less than one year, use part II of Form 4797, line 10. Your loss or gain will be the amount you sold the asset for, minus the amount you paid for the item. That number is carried over to line 14 of your 1040 and considered an ordinary loss or gain. It will *not* be figured into Section 1231 recapture in this, or future, years.

Business Use Drops Under 50%

If the item you claimed a Section 179 deduction on (or listed property you depreciated using an accelerated method) is no longer used at least 50% for business purposes, you should pay recapture taxes. List that item and figure its recapture in Part IV of Form 4797. You will pay recapture on the amount you have deducted, up to the amount the asset could have been depreciated using ADS. You will recapture it on the same form you originally took the deduction on (Schedule C, line 6).

Casualty and Theft (Form 4684) (p.147-148)

Casualty

A casualty loss is treated as a net operating loss (Chapter 14). A casualty is loss arising from a sudden, unexpected, or unusual cause (i.e. fire or flood). A gain could be recognized if you received insurance money for the item. However, you can make the election to use involuntary conversion rules and purchase a replacement with your insurance payout (within two years) to avoid tax consequences. The new item's basis is figured by: cost of new item, minus the tax basis of old item, plus any insurance not used, but received. If the item is only damaged, and later repaired, the amount spent to repair it is added to its basis.

If the item is insured, a timely insurance claim must be filed.

Theft

You may claim theft if your item was stolen, but not if you lost it or left it somewhere accidentally. You may not claim theft if there is an existing reimbursement claim for which there is a reasonable probability of recovery. As with casualties, you may only claim theft of an insured item if a timely insurance claim was filed.

Generally, the amount of casualty or theft losses you may claim is the tax basis of it immediately before the damage or loss occurred. The amount is further reduced by any insurance received.

See Publication 547 for more information.

Like-Kind Exchanges (Form 8824)(p. 152-153)

Generally, a like-kind exchange is a trade of one asset for another, which is of the same depreciation class. For the scope of this book, we will discuss what is commonly known as a trade-in. Property used for personal purposes does not fall under the like-kind exchange rules.

If you simply trade in your old equipment toward the purchase price of new, there is no tax consequence. The cost basis for the new equipment will be the tax basis left on the old, increased by any additional funds you paid for the new. This is figured on Form 8824, even though no loss or gain is recognized.

> **Example:** Sid traded in his old computer, which had a tax basis of $600 left on it, for a new computer. He paid $1000 to the store, in addition to trading in the old computer. His basis in the new computer for figuring gain, loss, or depreciation in future years is $1600. (600 + 1000 = 1600)

If cash is received by you, in addition to the asset you receive in return from your exchange, you may have realized a gain for the cash portion. (IRC 1031)

Abandonment

The business computer blew-up. You are taking it to the dump. You are surrendering it without passing it on to anyone else. You treat your adjusted basis in it as an ordinary loss, reported on Form 4797.

Note: Sales and exchanges between relatives have different rules. (IRC Section 267) See Publications 544 and 547 for more information on everything mentioned in this chapter.

Vehicles
Chapter 9

If you use your vehicle for obtaining inventory or supplies for your business, you may deduct the business percentage of your automobile expenses. You may also deduct any expenses incurred for the business use of a train, bus, or taxi used for local business travel. You will need to keep records to determine to what extent your car was driven for business purposes.

Mileage Records

Record your mileage. Make a habit of writing down the odometer reading on January 1 each year. You may use a spreadsheet like the example shown on the following page, or something as simple as a pocket calendar you keep in your glove box. Whatever the method, make sure to WRITE IT DOWN. Record your starting mileage, ending mileage, where you went, and the purpose of your trip. Jot down your mileage on a scrap of paper if you have to. When you return home, you can fill in the remaining information on your spreadsheet. Total how many miles you drove for business only—round trip. The remaining miles used on your vehicle this year are either personal or commuting. Vehicles are considered listed property, as discussed in Chapter 7. Therefore, you must keep records denoting business use.

Mileage Chart—Beginning Mileage January 1—98,047

Starting Mileage	Ending Mileage	Destination	Purpose	Date	Business Miles
98,047	98,098	Wrap Me Up	Purchase packaging materials	1/1/2007	51
98,098	98,110	Buy Cheap	Thrift store to buy inventory	1/2/2007	12
98,196	98,402	St. Louis	Antique sale to buy inventory	1/20/2007	206

If your office is in your home, you will not have any commuting mileage. If, however, you work in an office on Main Street, instead of your home, the number of miles between your house, that location, and back again are your commuting miles. Write the number of business, personal, and commuting miles down in the appropriate blanks on Part IV of your Schedule C. You figure your total mileage for the year by subtracting your odometer reading on January 1st, from the odometer reading at the end of the year.

You may either claim the Standard Mileage Rate (SMR) or Actual Expenses, not both in the same year. You need to keep records of your mileage, regardless. This is how you will figure the percentage you used your vehicle for business. During an audit, the IRS will expect to see your mileage records if you have taken any deduction or depreciation associated with your vehicle.

Standard Mileage Rate (SMR)

Taking the standard mileage rate (SMR) means you are able to deduct a certain amount for each business mile driven in a particular year (48.5 cents in 2007). You multiply the number of business miles driven by 48.5 cents (2007) per mile in order to figure your standard mileage rate deduction. This amount is figured in Part IV of your Schedule C, then deducted in Part II, line 9 of the same form. There are spaces to account for commuting and personal miles in Part IV, Schedule C, but they are not deductible.

You may also deduct the business percentage of parking fees and tolls, and the business percentage of state and local personal property taxes on the vehicle, in addition to the standard mileage rate. If you itemize your household deductions instead of taking the standard deduction, you may claim the remainder of your state and local personal property taxes on the vehicle on your Schedule A.

Example: Dawn drove her car a *total* of 4530 miles this year. She drove her car 453 *business* miles this year. She multiplies that number by 48.5 cents (453 x 48 and ½ cents = $219.70.) If she does not have any parking fees or personal property taxes to report on her car, she can simply carry $219.70 to line 9 of her Schedule C.

If she does have parking and state and local personal property taxes on her car, she will figure the business percentage she used her car by dividing the business miles by the total miles. (453÷4530 = 10%) Now, she will total her parking and state and local personal property taxes on her car.

If she paid out a total of $150 in parking fees, she will figure 10% of that by multiplying 150 x 10%. Dawn will be able to deduct $15 in addition to the $219.70 for the standard mileage rate. She will enter $234.70 on line 9, Schedule C.

If Dawn had a total of $200 in state and local personal property taxes for the vehicle, she will find her business percentage (200 x 10%). She may also deduct $20 on line 23 of her Schedule C.

If you want to use the standard mileage rate on a vehicle, you must choose it in the first year the automobile is available for use in your business. Then, in later years, you may choose to use either the standard mileage rate or actual expenses (discussed next). If you switch from the SMR to actual expenses and want to deduct depreciation, however, you must use straight-line depreciation, as opposed to an accelerated method, estimating the remaining useful life of the car.

When the SMR is NOT Allowed:

- You may not deduct mileage on a car for hire (taxi).
- You use five or more cars in your business at the same time.
- You claimed an accelerated depreciation method in previous years on the same car.
- You claimed a Section 179 deduction on the car.
- You claimed actual expenses on a car you leased after 1997.
- You are a rural mail carrier who received a qualified reimbursement.
- You claimed actual expenses on the same vehicle in the first year you used the automobile in your business.

Actual Expenses

To deduct the business percentage of your automobile expenses, keep receipts of your actual expenses. Gasoline, oil, tires, repairs, insurance, depreciation, parking fees and tolls, licenses, garage rent, lease payments, registration fees, and interest on car loans are all allowable deductions under the actual expense method. Total your receipts. Then figure out the percentage of those receipts you may claim based on the percentage the vehicle was used for business purposes. Use the mileage you tracked to figure the business percent the car was used. Divide the business mileage by the total mileage the car was driven for all purposes combined to arrive at your business percentage.

> **Example:** To figure how much of her actual expenses she may deduct, Olivia must keep track of the amount she used her car for business purposes. She drove a total of 20,000 miles this year. Of that 20,000 miles, 2000 of them were for business purposes.
> (2000/20,000 = 10%)
>
> Her receipt totals are:
> Gasoline = $4000
> Tires = $200
> Repairs = $650
> Insurance = $250
> Registration = $76
> Interest = $150
> Total = $5326 x 10% = $532.60
>
> Olivia may deduct $532.60 in actual expenses (line 9, Schedule C), plus depreciation this year.

As stated previously, using the actual expense method in the first year the vehicle is used for business keeps you from using the standard mileage method in later years.

Depreciation

Generally, business use of a vehicle is depreciated using the 200% declining balance (discussed in Chapter 7). However, if you use the car 50% or less for business purposes, or you used the standard mileage rate in a previous year on the same car, you must use straight-line depreciation. For those reasons, this book will not focus on accelerated depreciation of an automobile. It is more likely you will use your car 50% or less for online selling.

More information on depreciation of all types may be found in Publications 463 and 946.

Straight-Line Depreciation (Form 4562)

Figuring Basis

Begin by figuring the basis in your car. The purchase price, plus sales tax, is reduced by any salvage value and by any mileage you took using the standard mileage rate. If you used the SMR in previous years, you will need to reduce your basis by subtracting a certain amount per mile you've previously deducted on that vehicle. (17 cents for any miles deducted in 2005 or 2006—charts for other years are found in Publication 463) The *cost* of a car includes only cash paid (including sales tax) and does not include any amount of a trade-in allowance. Your *basis* for the new car, however, does include any amount left on the *basis* of the old car traded-in.

> **Example:** Jordan's basis in his car is $8000—what he paid to purchase it (plus sales tax.) He has owned the car for tax years 2005 and 2006. Thus far, he has only taken the standard mileage rate deduction on it.
>
> In 2005, he claimed 200 business miles. In 2006, he claimed 382 business miles. When Jordan is ready to sell the car, or wants to switch to straight-line depreciation, he will need to reduce his basis.   *continued*

2005 = 200 x 17 cents = $34.00
2006 = 382 x 17 cents = $64.94
Total = $98.94

Jordan must reduce his basis by $98.94. His new basis
is $7901.06. (8000 − 98.94 = $7901.06)

Using Straight-Line Depreciation

To use the straight-line method of depreciation for an automobile, you deduct your
business percentage of the basis equally over five calendar years. However, because
of the half-year convention, as explained in Chapter 7, you have to deduct only half
of the amount allowed in the first year. You may then continue to take the remaining percent in the sixth year on five year property.

Straight-Line Depreciation of 5-year Property
Year 1 = 10%
Year 2 = 20%
Year 3 = 20%
Year 4 = 20%
Year 5 = 20%
Year 6 = 10%

Limits!!

There are limits set as to the amount you may depreciate a vehicle each year. The
limits are also reduced to reflect your business percentage.

Limits for cars

Maximum deductions claimed for cars placed in service after 12/31/05 but before
01/01/07, based on 100% business use, are:

Year 1	Year 2	Year 3	Years 4 and up
$2960	$4800	$2850	$1775

Example: Cristy purchased a car for $19,800 this year. She uses it 40% for business purposes. She may depreciate the car by her business basis in it of $7920. (19,800 x 40% = 7920)

Using straight-line depreciation, she would be allowed to depreciate it evenly over a five year period ($1584 per year). Because of the half-year convention, however, she can only depreciate it by $792 this year. (Half of $1584 = $792) She can, therefore, continue to depreciate the vehicle into the sixth year to finish depreciating it.

Year 1 = $792   Year 4 = $1584
Year 2 = $1584   Year 5 = $1584
Year 3 = $1584   Year 6 = $792

Now, Cristy must check what she may depreciate each year against the depreciation limits for a car. She must reduce the limits by her business usage of the car. Let's assume it stays at 40%. Her depreciation limits become:

Year 1 (2960 x 40%) $1184
Year 2 (4800 x 40%) $1920
Year 3 (2850 x 40%) $1140
Years 4 and up (1775 x 40%) $710

Based on her limits, the amount of depreciation Cristy is allowed to take each year now looks like this:

Year 1 = $792
Year 2 = $1584
Year 3 = $1140
Year 4 = $710
Year 5 and up = $710

continued

At the end of the fifth year, Cristy will still have $2984 left to depreciate of the $7920 original business basis in the car. She may continue to depreciate the car by $710 each year until it is fully depreciated (but not below zero or the salvage value), until she disposes of it, or stops using it for business purposes—whichever comes first.

Limits for Trucks and Vans

The IRS understands there are higher costs associated with trucks and vans (including an SUV or minivan built on a truck chassis), so the limit is set higher for these types of vehicles. Maximum deductions claimed for trucks and vans, under 6000 pounds gross loaded weight, placed in service after 12/31/05 but before 01/01/07, based on 100% business use, are:

Year1	Year 2	Year 3	Years 4 and up
$3260	$5200	$3150	$1875

Electric Vehicles

Electric and certain other alternative fuel vehicles also have higher limits for depreciation than regular passenger cars. The limits for electric vehicles, placed in service after 12/31/05 but before 01/01/07, based on 100% business use, are:

Year1	Year 2	Year 3	Years 4 and up
$8980	$14,400	$8650	$5225

Section 179 Automobile

If you use your vehicle over 50% for business purposes, you may deduct its basis, plus sales tax, in the first year you place the car in service—if you use the actual expense method. You may only deduct the business percent of your basis. You are still limited by the maximum depreciation limit for your deduction ($2960, reduced by your business percentage of usage, the Section 179 limit, and your income as with other Section 179 property—Chapter 7) and must never use the standard mileage rate for that vehicle in the future.

Choosing Section 179 over depreciation for your vehicle deduction will generally only be beneficial if you are deducting the price of an inexpensive used car or have a heavy vehicle, as explained next.

Certain Other Vehicles

If you have put a vehicle into use in your business that has a gross weight when loaded of over 6000 pounds and under 14,000 pounds, it will fall under slightly different rules. (Check the manufacturer's specifications for gross loaded weight.)

Section 179 Heavy Vehicles

The Section 179 limit for such a vehicle rises to $25,000 (as opposed to the $2960 limit for regular cars and $3260 for trucks and vans).

Depreciation Heavy Vehicles

There is no yearly depreciation limit on such a vehicle.

Based on 100% business use, the percentages you may depreciate heavy vehicles are:

Year 1 – 5-20% (depending on month it was purchased.)
Year 2 – 32%
Year 3 – 19.2%
Year 4 – 11.52%
Year 5 – 11.52%
Year 6 – remaining percent to equal a total of 100.

Selling a Vehicle

Selling a vehicle works the same as selling your other section 1245, listed property, as explained in Chapter 8. Sale price – tax basis = loss or gain. Report only the business percentage as loss or gain. Reported and figured on Form 4797.

Trade-In

If you trade in a vehicle toward the purchase price of a new one, there is no tax consequence. Simply add the tax basis left on the old car to the money paid out for the new car. This will be the new car's tax basis. Reported on Form 8824.

Additional Notes:
Sales and Exchanges between relatives have different rules.

There may be additional credits for which you qualify if you drive an alternative fuel vehicle.

Depreciation and Section 179 deductions of a vehicle used in your business are figured on Form 4562 (p.145-146). Vehicles are considered listed property.

Business Use of Home
Chapter 10

(Form 8829)

What Qualifies as a Home Office

If you work from home, package, or store inventory there, even if you rent, you may claim that portion of some of your home expenses on your taxes—as long as it is your principal place of business. The portion of your home used must be used exclusively (can not also be used for personal purposes) and on a regular basis. A separate room is ideal, but may be a portion of a room if it is a clearly defined space. Just sticking a filing cabinet in the corner does NOT qualify. However, an entire side of the room occupied by your desk, computer, and packaging station can qualify if that area is never used for personal purposes. Separating that area with some sort of room divider will strengthen the argument that it is a separately identifiable space.

Inventory, however, may be stored in personal spaces as long as the space is used for inventory on a regular basis and is a separately identifiable space (the closet along with your clothes).

Calculating Business Percentage of Home

Let's assume you have devoted an entire room solely to your business. First, we figure out what percent of your home is used. (Even an unattached building, like a garage, qualifies.) Measure the square footage of the business area. Now, divide that number by the total square footage of your house (including business area).

> **Business Percentage of Home**
>
> If your room is 10x12 (120 sq. ft.) and your house is 1200 sq. ft., the business portion of your home is 10% (120÷1200). You may then deduct 10% of your mortgage interest, real estate taxes, insurance, utilities, repairs, security system, and maintenance.

If you rent, you can deduct the business percentage of your rent, utilities, and renter's insurance.

Direct and Indirect Expenses

When you fill out Form 8829, Part II, (p. 151) you will need to know whether your expenses are direct or indirect. For indirect expenses, you will list the full amount of the expense. The form will later direct you to reduce that amount to a business percentage.

Direct

Direct expenses relate directly to the business area of your home. If you paint or make repairs to only that area, those expenses are 100% deductible, up to your limit. (Limits are discussed later in this chapter.)

Indirect

Indirect expenses relate to the entire home. Insurance and utility bills are for the entire home. You may only deduct your business percentage of these expenses, up to your limit.

> **Example:** Adam paid $6000 in home mortgage interest this year. He used his home 20% for business. He will list $6000 on line 10 of Form 8829 under the indirect expenses column, since the interest was paid on the entire home. On line 13, he will be directed to multiply that $6000 by 20% (his business percentage). Adam may take a $1200 deduction for his home mortgage interest.

Casualty Losses—Can be direct, indirect, or non-deductible depending on which area of the home is affected. See instructions for Form 8829 for more information.

Insurance—Indirect—Only the business percentage of premiums paid and extending through the current tax year.

Security System—Indirect—Business portion of cost to maintain and monitor the system. The cost of the system itself can be depreciated.

Utilities and Services—Indirect—Business portion of utilities (and even maid service) may be deducted.

Rent—Indirect—Business percentage of rent.

Repairs—The cost of repairs relating only to the business portion of your home. They can be direct or indirect, depending on the repair. For instance, a new roof (or even a patch over the business area) is an indirect expense. Repairing a hole in the wall of your business area is direct.

Depreciation of Your Home

If you own your own home, you can also depreciate the home based on the percent used for business.

> **Things You Need to Know Before Depreciating:**
>
> - Date you began using home for business.
> - Adjusted basis and fair market value for home (excluding land) at the time you began using the home for business.
> - Cost of any improvements before and after you began using the home for business.
> - Percentage of your home used for business.

Find the adjusted basis of your home. (Cost or fair market value, plus permanent improvements, minus any casualty loss or depreciation taken in earlier years.) Take the adjusted basis of your home, not including land, and multiply it by the percentage used for business. You can depreciate the business portion of your home over 39 years using the MACRS straight-line method as nonresidential real property. You may only depreciate the house. You may never depreciate the land.

> **Using our 10% example:**
>
> Adjusted basis of house (not including land) = $120,000 x 10% (business percentage) = $12,000 (business basis)
>
> $12,000÷39 years = $307.69 depreciation amount per year.
>
> You must, however, adjust this amount (in the first year only) depending on which month you first used a portion of the home for business. This is called the mid-month convention.

First Year Depreciation on House Using the Mid-Month Convention

Go by the month you first used the home for business purposes. You may multiply your business basis of the adjusted basis of your home by:

January	2.461%
February	2.247%
March	2.033%
April	1.819%
May	1.605%
June	1.391%
July	1.177%
August	0.963%
September	0.749%
October	0.535%
November	0.321%
December	0.107%

The result is the amount you may depreciate your home in the first year you use it for business purposes.

Downside of Depreciation

When you sell your home, you may exclude $250,000 (individual) of the gain, as long as you have owned and lived in the home for more than two years. If you have taken deductions on your home, however, you may not exclude the deduction amounts from taxes.

The caveat to depreciating is that if you depreciate the business portion of your home, and later sell the house at a gain, you will have to pay taxes on the gain, up to the amount of any depreciation you deducted at a maximum tax rate of 25%. For more information on selling your home, see IRS Publication 523.

Limits

You are limited in the amount you may take for a home office deduction. Your limit is the total of:

> • Your tentative profit or loss from line 29, Schedule C,
> • Plus any net gain or loss from Schedule D,
> • Plus any net gain or loss from Form 4797

Carry-Over

You may carry-over any amount you were unable to take this year, to next year's Form 8829. However, you will still be limited by next year's business income, as well.

Part Year Use

If you only use your home for business during part of the year, you may only deduct that portion for home office expenses.

> **Example:** Kay began her online business in August. She may only deduct expenses from the date she created her home office in August, through the end of the year.
>
> This not only includes choosing August on the first year depreciation table for her home, but also all other expenses associated with the home office deduction. For instance, Kay may only deduct the business portion of her electric bill for the months of August, September, October, November, and December that year.

The total expenses from the business use of your home you are allowed to take are carried over to line 30 of Schedule C, after being figured on Form 8829 (p. 151).

See Publication 587 for more information on taking a home office deduction.

Employees
Chapter 11

You may get to the point in your online business where it becomes advantageous to hire employees to help. If you have grown to the point of full hiring mode, you should read IRS Publications 15 and 15A (Circular E—Employer's Tax Guide and Employer's Supplemental Tax Guide). The publications should be thoroughly studied when deciding to hire an employee.

Maybe, however, you just need assistance with packaging or scouting for items periodically. If this is the case, you may want to consider hiring your family members or an independent contractor, both of which are given space in this chapter. I will also touch on hiring regular employees.

Regular Employees

EIN

If you decide to hire an employee, you must first obtain an employer identification number (EIN). In order to receive an EIN, you will fill out and submit Form SS-4 (Application for EIN) (p.134). This part will not cost you anything.

Employee Paperwork

You will need to have each employee fill out Form I-9 (Employment Eligibility Verification) and Form W-4 (Employee's Withholding Allowance Certificate) (p.135). Also make sure you have their full name and Social Security number. These are forms you retain in your own files, rather than mailing them off to the IRS. The W-4 will assist you in figuring out how much to withhold from each employee's wages.

Withholding Payroll Taxes

You will be responsible for withholding an employee's payroll taxes from each check. These taxes consist of federal income tax, Social Security, and Medicare. You will only withhold half of the worker's Social Security and Medicare (FICA). Your business matches that and pays the other half. You will make deposits on the payroll taxes monthly or quarterly, depending on how much is owed. Assistance on how much to withhold is found in IRS Publications 15 and 15A.

In order to deposit the employee's taxes with the U.S. Treasury, you may use the Electronic Federal Tax Payment System (EFTPS) through the IRS website. Alternatively, you may take your deposit and Form 8109-B (Federal Deposit Coupon) to an authorized financial institution or a Federal Reserve bank serving your area.

Unemployment

Unemployment taxes must also be paid. These taxes, however, are paid by your business, not withheld from the employee's check. Unemployment taxes are paid and reported on Form 940 (Employer's Annual Federal Unemployment Tax Return) (p. 136-137).

Penalties

Payroll taxes must be filed on time. The IRS charges 2% for payments made even 1-5 days late. The rate only goes up from there. If you do not withhold, or make payments on, your employee's payroll taxes, your business, and therefore you as a sole proprietor, are liable for those taxes and additional penalties. The IRS penalties can be severe for failure to withhold and/or pay.

Most states also require tax withholding. All states require unemployment taxes. Check with your local and state agencies for more information. (www.taxesforonlinesellers.com)

Other Forms and Due Dates

In addition to making payroll tax deposits and filing unemployment, employers must also file other forms. Form 941 (Employer's Quarterly Federal Tax Return) (p.138-139) is filed quarterly. If you owe withheld taxes of under $1000, you will file Form 944 (Employer's Annual Federal Tax Return) (p. 140-141) instead of Form 941. It is filed by January 31 for the preceding year. You must also mail a W-2 to your employee by January 31.

By February 28, you will need to mail a Form W-3 (Transmittal of Wage and Tax Statements), plus a copy of the employee's W-2 to the IRS. Also by February 28, you must mail copies of the W-2 and W-3 to the Social Security Administration.

You must keep copies and records of EVERYTHING!

Independent Contractors

Responsibilities

If you hire an independent contractor, you do not have to withhold or report payroll taxes, FICA, or unemployment. The only things, tax wise, you have to do each year are to issue a Form 1099MISC to the independent contractor, a copy to the IRS, and a Form 1096 (Annual Summary and Transmittal of U.S. Information Returns) to the IRS. All of these must be sent by January 31. You only have to do those things if you paid the contractor $600 or more for the previous year, and the payment was for business, not personal, reasons. They are responsible for their own taxes and are treated as business owners, themselves, when filing their own Schedule C.

First and foremost, make certain that your independent contractor is truly considered such by the IRS. Be careful about misidentifying an employee as an independent contractor. If the IRS decides you have misrepresented an employee in this manner, they may not only make you pay that person's employment taxes, but can penalize you an additional percent of those taxes.

Create a written agreement, signed by both you and the worker, stating he is an independent contractor. It should also spell out the terms of your business agreement. For instance, that he will work off site, not have taxes withheld, and get paid by the job, reported on a Form 1099.

Keep records of:

- The worker's name, address, and social security number
- Dates worked if applicable
- Amounts paid and the job done
- Any expenses paid by you for the worker
- Copies of all 1099's and other tax forms

Some factors that go into determining whether your worker qualifies as an independent contractor are:

- Independent Contractors
- Can set their own work hours,
- Have little training by you,
- Do not work full-time for you,
- Can hire someone else to do the work for them if they choose,
- Can quit when they choose,
- Don't work for you every day,
- Can work on location or elsewhere if they choose,
- Generally decide when the work will be done,
- Are not required to submit reports,
- Are paid by the job, not by the hour/week/month,
- Are not reimbursed specifically for expenses,
- Provide own equipment and supplies,
- Can realize a profit or loss as a result of services,
- May work for others at the same time,
- Cannot be fired as long as they produce the requested work,
- May have their own business license.

(Not all of these things have to be the case, but the more that apply to your worker, the better.)

Hiring Your Family

Children

You may hire even your minor children as long as you give them real work to do, and the pay is a fair market wage. You cannot pay your son $50 per hour to package, no matter how creative he is with tape. He *could*, however, earn $8 per hour.

A minor child can earn up to $5150 (2006) each year without owing taxes to the IRS. Then, as long as the income is earned by a child who works for a parent, the tax rate starts at 10%. Besides the lower tax rate, no Social Security, Medicare, or unemployment taxes are due when the child (under 18 for SS and Medicare, under 21 for unemployment) works for his parent's business (sole proprietor or partnership). Your child's wages are subject to income tax withholding rules, regardless of age.

You will still qualify for the Child Tax Credit as long as your employed child did not pay for more than half of his own support throughout the year.

A job description should be written out, along with an agreed upon rate of pay. You should keep a written record of hours worked. A fourteen year old is quite capable of assisting you at sales, researching items, or other administrative tasks. Your seventeen year old may deliver your packages to the post office each day. Even your eight year old can help with packaging.

The money your children earn from your business is considered earned income. This means they will avoid the kiddie tax (unless they have additional, unearned/investment income).

Spouse

When you hire your spouse in the business, everything works exactly the same way as when hiring a regular employee, except you do not have to pay federal unemployment taxes on a spouse. This could work to your advantage, or it could work against you. The Social Security and Medicare paid will total 15.3%. State unemployment and disability requirements may cost more than it saves to put a spouse on the payroll. Let them volunteer, instead.

Parents

Hiring your parents in your business works the same way as hiring a spouse. You must withhold payroll taxes, but do not have to pay federal unemployment. Make sure you are not reducing an older parent's Social Security benefits before putting them on the payroll.

More information may be found in Publications 15 and 15A for information concerning hiring all types of workers.

Self-Employment Taxes
Chapter 12

(Schedule SE)

What is Self-Employment Tax?

Self-employment tax is comprised of the Social Security (12.4%) and Medicare (2.9%) payments for yourself. It is based on your net earnings from self-employment. This means it is figured after all of your business expenses have been deducted. The more you are able to get your net profit number down with honest deductions, the less self-employment tax you will pay.

Who Must File?

You must file Schedule SE, Self-Employment Tax (p. 133), if you had net earnings from self-employment of $400 or more in a given tax year. Even if you had less than $400 in self-employment income, it may be to your advantage to file Schedule C, as stated earlier in the book. If, with deductions, you get your self-employment income down to a loss (discussed in Chapter 14), you may be able to offset other income earned by you or your spouse. If you have made quarterly, estimated payments (discussed in Chapter 13), you may be due a refund.

Where to File

As an online seller, you should generally be able to use Section A—Short Schedule SE, which is self-explanatory and quite simple to fill out. Once you figure your SE tax, you may deduct half of it on your 1040, line 27, in order to figure your total adjusted gross income.

When You Can't Pay Your Taxes Due

When you cannot pay your taxes due, the IRS may allow you an extension, or the opportunity to set up a payment plan. As long as you do not pay, interest and penalties will be added. The key here is to contact them quickly. Do not hide from it and hope not to be found.

For more information, see the IRS instructions for Schedule SE.

Filing Quarterly
Chapter 13

(Form 1040ES)

When and What to Pay

Four times per year, you must pay estimated taxes on your income and self-employment tax. Due dates for these payments are: April 15, June 15, September 15, and January 15. You are supposed to estimate (guess) the amount of income you will earn and subsequent taxes you will owe for the entire year. Self-employment tax must be taken into consideration when figuring estimated payments. You need to then pay 25% of this amount quarterly.

Tax software generally figures your estimated taxes based on what you did in previous years. It can also prepare estimated forms for you.

If you are not liable for paying estimated taxes prior to a given due date, but become liable before the next due date, file for the quarter you become liable, but increase your percentage paid.

Example: Dan has a regular job through which taxes are withheld from each paycheck. He begins selling online. During the first part of the year, he is having enough taxes already withheld to cover his online income, as well as his regular income.

In July, however, Dan's online sales spike significantly. He realizes the amount withheld from his regular paycheck will no longer cover his total tax liability. He may file a Form 1040ES by September 15, paying 75% (75% - because it is the third quarter) of his estimated tax due without realizing penalties.

Dan may also be able to increase the amount he has withheld from his regular paycheck, instead of having to file estimated payments.

Exceptions to Paying Estimated Taxes:
- You expect to owe less than $1000 for the year, after subtracting taxes withheld from other employment,
- AND, You expect your withheld taxes to be the smaller of (1) 90% of your total taxes for the year, or (2) 100% of your total taxes for the previous year.

If you and/or your spouse has income tax withheld from a paycheck, no estimated taxes are due if the withheld taxes cover more than 90% of the total tax bill for that year—or—if the tax withheld totals more than your entire tax bill from the previous year.

This means if you (and/or your spouse if married filing jointly) is an employee at another job besides the business, just make sure they/you are having enough tax withheld from their/your check to cover taxes due from your business income, too. If so, you can forget about making estimated, quarterly payments. In essence, that withholding is paying your quarterly business payments, as well as the taxes due on the other earned income.

IRS Publication 919 will help you compare the total tax to be withheld during the year with the tax you can expect to figure on your return. It will also help you determine how much additional withholding you may need each payday from your regular job in order to avoid owing taxes and penalties for not filing quarterly. To add to the amount withheld from your regular job, you'll need to fill out a new W-4 for your employer.

Form 1040ES

Form 1040ES (p.142) is a simple payment voucher where you list your and your spouse's names, social security numbers, and address. The only other space on the form is to write in the amount you are paying. Don't forget to include a check.

There is a worksheet to help you figure your estimated tax in the instruction booklet for 1040ES.

If you earn *under* $150,000, quarterly payments must equal 90% of your final income tax bill or at least 100% of last years tax bill (amt. due before deducting what had already been paid—line 63 of 1040).

If you earn *over* $150,000, you must pay at least 110% of last year's tax bill, spread out quarterly, or risk an under-payment penalty.

Overpayment

If you over-pay your estimated taxes and expect a refund, you may elect to apply it to next year's estimated payments.

Underpayment and Late Payments

You could receive a tax penalty if you under-pay or miss a deadline. If you are late, you could also end up paying interest on what you owe. Your state may require quarterly payments, as well.

NOL—Net Operating Loss
Chapter 14

Net Operating Loss

What if you get the bottom of your Schedule C, and the remaining number is negative? This means you have a net operating loss (NOL), or lost money in your business venture this year. Your business deductions totaled more than your business income. The IRS understands that businesses, especially in their start-up years, may not always make a profit.

At Risk

The first thing you will notice when you end up with a negative number on your Schedule C is that it directs you to check either box 32a or box 32b. What does this mean? Unless you borrowed money for the business under a situation stating you do not have to pay it back in the event the business fails, you may check box 32a. All of your investment is at risk—even if you borrowed no money at all.

Carry-Back and Carry-Forward of NOL

If you have a net operating loss (NOL), it is used to then offset other income made by you (and/or your spouse if married filing jointly) on your 1040. You may not, however, reduce your total taxable income below zero with a net operating loss. Instead, you may use the remaining NOL to offset income made in the previous two years by filing amended returns. If you still have left-over NOL amounts after carrying them back two years, you may carry them forward for future years' tax returns. You may carry them forward for up to twenty years, or until they are completely used. Carry-over amounts do not count against you in the 3 out of 5 rule discussed later. They are only counted for the year incurred. Use form 3621 (Net Operating Loss Carry Over).

> **Example:** Laura sells glass apples on eBay. The first year she was in business, she spent a great deal of money setting up shop. She bought equipment and supplies to use in business. She traveled around the country obtaining her inventory. Sales were good that first year, but she still ended up, after deductions, having a net operating loss of $40,000. Laura's husband worked for the local newspaper company. Bill earned $30,000.
>
> Laura and Bill may use the $40,000 to offset Bill's $30,000 income. They are left with $10,000 of unused NOL from the first year, which may be carried-back, and then forward. If their tax bill was not zero or less in the two previous years, they must file an amended return for each of those years in order to receive a refund using the $10,000.
>
> If, after carrying-back their NOL, there is any left over, they may continue to carry it forward. Let's say, after carrying it back, Laura and Bill still had an unused NOL amount of $6,000. During Laura's second year in business, she made a profit of $13,000. She may then
>
> *continued*

use her previous, unused NOL amount to offset a portion of that $13,000 profit. Now, Laura will only have to pay taxes on $7,000 business income in the second year of business.

Hobby or Business

If you make a profit, you are in business. If you continuously lose money, however, you risk having your business activity classified as a hobby. The IRS sets several guidelines to determine whether they think you are a business or indulging your hobby at a discount. You do not necessarily have to make money, but must show you are making an honest effort to do so.

3 Out of 5 Rule

One thing the IRS looks at to determine your intentions is to examine the past five years of your business. If you have made profit in three out of five consecutive years, the IRS considers your venture a legitimate business. However, this is not the only thing the IRS studies.

If you fail the 3 out of 5 rule, but can still prove you are actively pursuing profit, you can still be classified as a business. Ways to do this include advertising, keeping good business records, past success in a similar business, having a business license, courses taken to improve your skills, and if this is your sole source of potential income, because that proves financial need.

Things You Can Do

As an online seller, you can attempt to show an effort at making profit in a variety of ways. First and foremost is keeping good business records. If you have an envelope stuffed full of receipts, or even receipts missing, you will not look like a professional business. If, however, you are documenting everything on spreadsheets, running an analysis (easily done with accounting software), and keeping your records in organized folders, you look much more like a legitimate business. Having a separate bank account used only for business purposes is rather important in showing business motive. As a sole proprietor, you can even have the bank account in your own name instead of the business name. Just make sure to keep the finances in the account only for business.

If you are having business cards printed as a means of advertising your business, or sending out catalogs of inventory to potential customers, you are actively seeking income. Purchasing books about online selling or attending something like eBay University will do even more to prove your intention of running a profitable business.

Why Does it Exist?

The hobby rule exists to keep people from indulging their hobbies by offsetting their other income with business losses. As an online seller, you may be overly confident you will automatically continue to be classified a business. After all, you are in the business of "sales." Picture for a moment a bookseller the IRS may assume is an avid reader. Think of the guy who sells baseball cards. Maybe he is selling off extraneous cards while trying to complete his collection. Then, there is always a seller who is in it just to be able to buy personal items at wholesale costs. This isn't legal and does not work, but there are those who try it anyway.

Worst Case Scenario

In the worst case scenario, the IRS tried to classify you as a hobbyist. You were audited and failed. You went one step further to appeal in tax court and still failed (which isn't likely for a true online seller, by the way). In the worst case scenario, your business is classified as a hobby—no ifs, ands, or buts. In this case, not all is lost. You may then still deduct some of your expenses, as long as those expenses do not create a loss.

> **Example:** Kevin, whose venture of selling his extra baseball cards while trying to complete his own collection, made $200 through eBay this year.
>
> Kevin had a total of $350 worth of expenses from traveling to baseball card shows, postage from mailing the items he sold, eBay fees, and sleeves to protect the cards. He may deduct $200 of those expenses as a hobbyist.
>
> Kevin may totally offset his income from the venture, but may not use a loss to offset any other current or future income.

Additional Notes:

The deductions you may take for hobby expenses are subject to the 2% floor on miscellaneous deductions as with other itemized, miscellaneous, personal deductions. This means deductions are allowed only to the extent that their total exceeds 2% of your Adjusted Gross Income on your 1040, along with other personal miscellaneous deductions on your Schedule A. You must file Schedule A (p.128) instead of taking the standard deduction in order to claim hobby expenses. Your hobby expenses are deducted on line 22 of your Schedule A (other expenses). Hobby income is reported on line 21 of your 1040 (other income).

See Publication 536 for more information on Net Operating Losses.

State and Local Taxes
Chapter 15

Be aware of state and local taxes. Most states impose a multitude of taxes and fees, many of which you may not be aware. It would be impossible for me to cover every state and their individual laws and regulations in this book. I will, however, mention some common things you should watch out for, and give you a link to find out more about your particular state.

State Sales Tax
In most states, you are responsible for paying sales tax on items purchased by a buyer living in your home state, whether or not you collected sales tax from the buyer.

Inventory and Equipment
Some states impose a tax on property used for the business.

Payroll Taxes
If your state has an income tax, you will not only have to pay taxes on your income, but also that of your employees.

Unemployment Taxes

All states have unemployment taxes.

License Fees

The cost of a business license or other permit may be mandatory in your state. A state tax ID number is essential to apply for if you buy from legitimate wholesalers.

Out-of-State Payroll Taxes

If you hire an employee who lives in another state, you will be responsible for withholding and paying his state payroll taxes in his home state.

Find your state agencies at: www.taxesforonlinesellers.com

Appendix

The forms on the following pages are to be used for reference while reading this book only and are not to be printed, copied, or filed. The resolution is not the best, and some of them may be hard to read, reduced to the print size required by this book. For a better visual, these forms, and more, may all be found at www.irs.gov in PDF format, or link to them from www.taxesforonlinesellers.com.

Most of the following forms have two book pages associated with them (front and back of the actual form). Usually, you can tell which form you are looking at by a notation in either the top left or bottom right corner.

Some of the following forms are dated 2006 and some are dated 2007. They represent the most current forms available for download at the time this book went to press.

Form **1040**

Department of the Treasury—Internal Revenue Service

U.S. Individual Income Tax Return **2006** (99) IRS Use Only—Do not write or staple in this space.

For the year Jan. 1–Dec. 31, 2006, or other tax year beginning , 2006, ending , 20

OMB No. 1545-0074

Label (See instructions on page 16.) **Use the IRS label. Otherwise, please print or type.**

Your first name and initial | Last name | Your social security number

If a joint return, spouse's first name and initial | Last name | Spouse's social security number

Home address (number and street). If you have a P.O. box, see page 16. | Apt. no.

City, town or post office, state, and ZIP code. If you have a foreign address, see page 16.

▲ You **must** enter your SSN(s) above. ▲

Checking a box below will not change your tax or refund.

Presidential Election Campaign ► Check here if you, or your spouse if filing jointly, want $3 to go to this fund (see page 16) ► ☐ You ☐ Spouse

Filing Status

Check only one box.

1 ☐ Single
2 ☐ Married filing jointly (even if only one had income)
3 ☐ Married filing separately. Enter spouse's SSN above and full name here. ►
4 ☐ Head of household (with qualifying person). (See page 17.) If the qualifying person is a child but not your dependent, enter this child's name here. ►
5 ☐ Qualifying widow(er) with dependent child (see page 17)

Exemptions

6a ☐ **Yourself.** If someone can claim you as a dependent, **do not** check box 6a
b ☐ **Spouse**
c **Dependents:**

(1) First name Last name	(2) Dependent's social security number	(3) Dependent's relationship to you	(4)✔ if qualifying child for child tax credit (see page 19)
			☐
			☐
			☐
			☐

If more than four dependents, see page 19.

d Total number of exemptions claimed

Boxes checked on 6a and 6b
No. of children on 6c who:
• **lived with you**
• did not live with you due to divorce or separation (see page 20)
Dependents on 6c not entered above
Add numbers on lines above ►

Income

Attach Form(s) W-2 here. Also attach Forms W-2G and 1099-R if tax was withheld.

If you did not get a W-2, see page 23.

Enclose, but do not attach, any payment. Also, please use Form 1040-V.

7	Wages, salaries, tips, etc. Attach Form(s) W-2	7
8a	**Taxable interest.** Attach Schedule B if required	8a
b	**Tax-exempt** interest. **Do not** include on line 8a	8b
9a	Ordinary dividends. Attach Schedule B if required	9a
b	Qualified dividends (see page 23)	9b
10	Taxable refunds, credits, or offsets of state and local income taxes (see page 24)	10
11	Alimony received	11
12	Business income or (loss). Attach Schedule C or C-EZ	12
13	Capital gain or (loss). Attach Schedule D if required. If not required, check here ► ☐	13
14	Other gains or (losses). Attach Form 4797	14
15a	IRA distributions 15a	b Taxable amount (see page 25)	15b
16a	Pensions and annuities 16a	b Taxable amount (see page 26)	16b
17	Rental real estate, royalties, partnerships, S corporations, trusts, etc. Attach Schedule E	17
18	Farm income or (loss). Attach Schedule F	18
19	Unemployment compensation	19
20a	Social security benefits 20a	b Taxable amount (see page 27)	20b
21	Other income. List type and amount (see page 29)	21
22	Add the amounts in the far right column for lines 7 through 21. This is your **total income** ►	22

Adjusted Gross Income

23	Archer MSA deduction. Attach Form 8853	23
24	Certain business expenses of reservists, performing artists, and fee-basis government officials. Attach Form 2106 or 2106-EZ	24
25	Health savings account deduction. Attach Form 8889	25
26	Moving expenses. Attach Form 3903	26
27	One-half of self-employment tax. Attach Schedule SE	27
28	Self-employed SEP, SIMPLE, and qualified plans	28
29	Self-employed health insurance deduction (see page 29)	29
30	Penalty on early withdrawal of savings	30
31a	Alimony paid b Recipient's SSN ►	31a
32	IRA deduction (see page 31)	32
33	Student loan interest deduction (see page 33)	33
34	Jury duty pay you gave to your employer	34
35	Domestic production activities deduction. Attach Form 8903	35
36	Add lines 23 through 31a and 32 through 35	36
37	Subtract line 36 from line 22. This is your **adjusted gross income** ►	37

For Disclosure, Privacy Act, and Paperwork Reduction Act Notice, see page 80. Cat. No. 11320B Form **1040** (2006)

Form 1040 (2006)   Page **2**

Tax and Credits	38	Amount from line 37 (adjusted gross income)	38
	39a	Check if: ☐ **You** were born before January 2, 1942, ☐ Blind. ☐ **Spouse** was born before January 2, 1942, ☐ Blind. } **Total boxes checked ▶ 39a**	
Standard Deduction for—	b	If your spouse itemizes on a separate return or you were a dual-status alien, see page 34 and check here ▶39b ☐	
	40	**Itemized deductions** (from Schedule A) **or** your **standard deduction** (see left margin) . .	40
	41	Subtract line 40 from line 38	41
• People who checked any box on line 39a or 39b **or** who can be claimed as a dependent, see page 34.	42	If line 38 is over $112,875, or you provided housing to a person displaced by Hurricane Katrina, see page 36. Otherwise, multiply $3,300 by the total number of exemptions claimed on line 6d	42
	43	**Taxable income.** Subtract line 42 from line 41. If line 42 is more than line 41, enter -0-	43
	44	**Tax** (see page 36). Check if any tax is from: a ☐ Form(s) 8814 b ☐ Form 4972 . . .	44
	45	**Alternative minimum tax** (see page 39). Attach Form 6251	45
• All others:	46	Add lines 44 and 45 . . . . ▶	46
Single or Married filing separately, $5,150	47	Foreign tax credit. Attach Form 1116 if required . . .	47	
	48	Credit for child and dependent care expenses. Attach Form 2441	48	
Married filing jointly or Qualifying widow(er), $10,300	49	Credit for the elderly or the disabled. Attach Schedule R .	49	
	50	Education credits. Attach Form 8863	50	
	51	Retirement savings contributions credit. Attach Form 8880 .	51	
	52	Residential energy credits. Attach Form 5695 . . .	52	
Head of household, $7,550	53	Child tax credit (see page 42). Attach Form 8901 if required	53	
	54	Credits from: a ☐ Form 8396 b ☐ Form 8839 c ☐ Form 8859	54	
	55	Other credits: a ☐ Form 3800 b ☐ Form 8801 c ☐ Form ___	55	
	56	Add lines 47 through 55. These are your **total credits**	56
	57	Subtract line 56 from line 46. If line 56 is more than line 46, enter -0- . . ▶	57
Other Taxes	58	Self-employment tax. Attach Schedule SE	58
	59	Social security and Medicare tax on tip income not reported to employer. Attach Form 4137 . .	59
	60	Additional tax on IRAs, other qualified retirement plans, etc. Attach Form 5329 if required . .	60
	61	Advance earned income credit payments from Form(s) W-2, box 9	61
	62	Household employment taxes. Attach Schedule H	62
	63	Add lines 57 through 62. This is your **total tax** . . . . ▶	63
Payments	64	Federal income tax withheld from Forms W-2 and 1099 . .	64	
	65	2006 estimated tax payments and amount applied from 2005 return	65	
If you have a qualifying child, attach Schedule EIC.	66a	Earned income credit (EIC)	66a	
	b	Nontaxable combat pay election ▶	66b	
	67	Excess social security and tier 1 RRTA tax withheld (see page 60)	67	
	68	Additional child tax credit. Attach Form 8812	68	
	69	Amount paid with request for extension to file (see page 60)	69	
	70	Payments from: a ☐ Form 2439 b ☐ Form 4136 c ☐ Form 8885 .	70	
	71	Credit for federal telephone excise tax paid. Attach Form 8913 if required	71	
	72	Add lines 64, 65, 66a, and 67 through 71. These are your **total payments** . . . . ▶	72
Refund Direct deposit? See page 61 and fill in 74b, 74c, and 74d, or Form 8888.	73	If line 72 is more than line 63, subtract line 63 from line 72. This is the amount you **overpaid**	73
	74a	Amount of line 73 you want **refunded to you.** If Form 8888 is attached, check here ▶ ☐	74a
	▶ b	Routing number	▶ c Type: ☐ Checking ☐ Savings	
	▶ d	Account number		
	75	Amount of line 73 you want **applied to your 2007 estimated tax** ▶	75	
Amount You Owe	76	**Amount you owe.** Subtract line 72 from line 63. For details on how to pay, see page 62 ▶	76
	77	Estimated tax penalty (see page 62)	77	

Third Party Designee
Do you want to allow another person to discuss this return with the IRS (see page 63)? ☐ **Yes.** Complete the following. ☐ **No**

| Designee's name ▶ | Phone no. ▶ ( ) | Personal identification number (PIN) ▶ | |

Sign Here
Joint return? See page 17.
Keep a copy for your records.

Under penalties of perjury, I declare that I have examined this return and accompanying schedules and statements, and to the best of my knowledge and belief, they are true, correct, and complete. Declaration of preparer (other than taxpayer) is based on all information of which preparer has any knowledge.

| Your signature | Date | Your occupation | Daytime phone number ( ) |
| Spouse's signature. If a joint return, **both** must sign. | Date | Spouse's occupation | |

Paid Preparer's Use Only

Preparer's signature ▶	Date	Check if self-employed ☐	Preparer's SSN or PTIN
Firm's name (or yours if self-employed), address, and ZIP code ▶		EIN	
		Phone no. ( )	

Form **1040** (2006)

SCHEDULES A&B
(Form 1040)

Department of the Treasury
Internal Revenue Service   (99)

Schedule A—Itemized Deductions

(Schedule B is on back)

▶ **Attach to Form 1040.**   ▶ **See Instructions for Schedules A&B (Form 1040).**

OMB No. 1545-0074

2006

Attachment
Sequence No. **07**

Name(s) shown on Form 1040

Your social security number

Sch. A

Medical and Dental Expenses		**Caution.** Do not include expenses reimbursed or paid by others.	
	1	Medical and dental expenses (see page A-1) . . .	1
	2	Enter amount from Form 1040, line 38 ⌊ 2 ⌋	
	3	Multiply line 2 by 7.5% (.075)	3
	4	Subtract line 3 from line 1. If line 3 is more than line 1, enter -0-	4
Taxes You Paid	5	State and local income taxes	5
	6	Real estate taxes (see page A-3)	6
(See page A-3.)	7	Personal property taxes	7
	8	Other taxes. List type and amount ▶..................	
			8
	9	Add lines 5 through 8	9
Interest You Paid	10	Home mortgage interest and points reported to you on Form 1098	10
	11	Home mortgage interest not reported to you on Form 1098. If paid to the person from whom you bought the home, see page A-3 and show that person's name, identifying no., and address ▶	
(See page A-3.)		....	
Note. Personal interest is not deductible.		....	11
	12	Points not reported to you on Form 1098. See page A-4 for special rules	12
	13	Investment interest. Attach Form 4952 if required. (See page A-4.)	13
	14	Add lines 10 through 13	14
Gifts to Charity	15	Gifts by cash or check. If you made any gift of $250 or more, see page A-5	15
If you made a gift and got a benefit for it, see page A-4.	16	Other than by cash or check. If any gift of $250 or more, see page A-5. You **must** attach Form 8283 if over $500	16
	17	Carryover from prior year	17
	18	Add lines 15 through 17	18
Casualty and Theft Losses	19	Casualty or theft loss(es). Attach Form 4684. (See page A-6.)	19
Job Expenses and Certain Miscellaneous Deductions	20	Unreimbursed employee expenses—job travel, union dues, job education, etc. Attach Form 2106 or 2106-EZ if required. (See page A-6.) ▶	20
	21	Tax preparation fees	21
(See page A-6.)	22	Other expenses—investment, safe deposit box, etc. List type and amount ▶..................	
			22
	23	Add lines 20 through 22	23
	24	Enter amount from Form 1040, line 38 ⌊ 24 ⌋	
	25	Multiply line 24 by 2% (.02)	25
	26	Subtract line 25 from line 23. If line 25 is more than line 23, enter -0-	26
Other Miscellaneous Deductions	27	Other—from list on page A-7. List type and amount ▶	
		....	27
Total Itemized Deductions	28	Is Form 1040, line 38, over $150,500 (over $75,250 if married filing separately)?	
		☐ **No.** Your deduction is not limited. Add the amounts in the far right column for lines 4 through 27. Also, enter this amount on Form 1040, line 40. ⎫ ▶	28
		☐ **Yes.** Your deduction may be limited. See page A-7 for the amount to enter. ⎭	
	29	If you elect to itemize deductions even though they are less than your standard deduction, check here ▶ ☐	

For Paperwork Reduction Act Notice, see Form 1040 instructions.   Cat. No. 11330X   **Schedule A (Form 1040) 2006**

SCHEDULE C
(Form 1040)

Department of the Treasury
Internal Revenue Service (99)

Profit or Loss From Business
(Sole Proprietorship)

▶ Partnerships, joint ventures, etc., must file Form 1065 or 1065-B.

▶ Attach to Form 1040, 1040NR, or 1041. ▶ See Instructions for Schedule C (Form 1040).

OMB No. 1545-0074

2006

Attachment
Sequence No. **09**

Name of proprietor

Social security number (SSN)

A Principal business or profession, including product or service (see page C-2 of the instructions)

B Enter code from pages C-8, 9, & 10
▶

C Business name. If no separate business name, leave blank.

D Employer ID number (EIN), if any

E Business address (including suite or room no.) ▶
City, town or post office, state, and ZIP code

F Accounting method: **(1)** ☐ Cash **(2)** ☐ Accrual **(3)** ☐ Other (specify) ▶

G Did you "materially participate" in the operation of this business during 2006? If "No," see page C-3 for limit on losses   ☐ Yes ☐ No

H If you started or acquired this business during 2006, check here   .   .   .   .   ▶ ☐

Part I   Income

1	Gross receipts or sales. **Caution.** If this income was reported to you on Form W-2 and the "Statutory employee" box on that form was checked, see page C-3 and check here . . . . . . ▶ ☐	1
2	Returns and allowances	2
3	Subtract line 2 from line 1	3
4	Cost of goods sold (from line 42 on page 2)	4
5	**Gross profit.** Subtract line 4 from line 3.	5
6	Other income, including federal and state gasoline or fuel tax credit or refund (see page C-3) .	6
7	**Gross income.** Add lines 5 and 6 . . . . ▶	7

Part II   Expenses. Enter expenses for business use of your home **only** on line 30.

8	Advertising	8	18	Office expense	18
9	Car and truck expenses (see page C-4)	9	19	Pension and profit-sharing plans	19
10	Commissions and fees .	10	20	Rent or lease (see page C-5):	
11	Contract labor (see page C-4)	11	**a**	Vehicles, machinery, and equipment	20a
12	Depletion	12	**b**	Other business property . .	20b
13	Depreciation and section 179 expense deduction (not included in Part III) (see page C-4)	13	21	Repairs and maintenance . .	21
			22	Supplies (not included in Part III)	22
			23	Taxes and licenses . . .	23
			24	Travel, meals, and entertainment:	
14	Employee benefit programs (other than on line 19). .	14	**a**	Travel	24a
15	Insurance (other than health) .	15	**b**	Deductible meals and entertainment (see page C-6)	24b
16	Interest:		25	Utilities	25
a	Mortgage (paid to banks, etc.) .	16a	26	Wages (less employment credits) .	26
b	Other	16b	27	Other expenses (from line 48 on page 2)	27
17	Legal and professional services	17			

28	**Total expenses** before expenses for business use of home. Add lines 8 through 27 in columns . ▶	28
29	Tentative profit (loss). Subtract line 28 from line 7	29
30	Expenses for business use of your home. Attach **Form 8829**	30
31	**Net profit or (loss).** Subtract line 30 from line 29.	
	● If a profit, enter on both **Form 1040, line 12**, and **Schedule SE, line 2**, or on **Form 1040NR, line 13** (statutory employees, see page C-6). Estates and trusts, enter on Form 1041, line 3.	31
	● If a loss, you **must** go to line 32.	
32	If you have a loss, check the box that describes your investment in this activity (see page C-6).	
	● If you checked 32a, enter the loss on both **Form 1040, line 12**, and **Schedule SE, line 2**, or on **Form 1040NR, line 13** (statutory employees, see page C-6). Estates and trusts, enter on Form 1041, line 3.	**32a** ☐ All investment is at risk. **32b** ☐ Some investment is not at risk.
	● If you checked 32b, you **must** attach **Form 6198.** Your loss may be limited.	

For Paperwork Reduction Act Notice, see page C-8 of the instructions.   Cat. No. 11334P   Schedule C (Form 1040) 2006

Sch. C

Sch. C

Part III   **Cost of Goods Sold** (see page C-7)

33	Method(s) used to value closing inventory: **a** ☐ Cost **b** ☐ Lower of cost or market **c** ☐ Other (attach explanation)		
34	Was there any change in determining quantities, costs, or valuations between opening and closing inventory? If "Yes," attach explanation . . . . ☐ Yes ☐ No
35	Inventory at beginning of year. If different from last year's closing inventory, attach explanation . .	**35**	
36	Purchases less cost of items withdrawn for personal use	**36**	
37	Cost of labor. Do not include any amounts paid to yourself	**37**	
38	Materials and supplies	**38**	
39	Other costs	**39**	
40	Add lines 35 through 39	**40**	
41	Inventory at end of year	**41**	
42	**Cost of goods sold.** Subtract line 41 from line 40. Enter the result here and on page 1, line 4 . . .	**42**	

Part IV   **Information on Your Vehicle.** Complete this part **only** if you are claiming car or truck expenses on line 9 and are not required to file Form 4562 for this business. See the instructions for line 13 on page C-4 to find out if you must file Form 4562.

43   When did you place your vehicle in service for business purposes? (month, day, year) ▶ ..../........../........

44   Of the total number of miles you drove your vehicle during 2006, enter the number of miles you used your vehicle for:

a Business ....   **b** Commuting (see instructions) ....   **c** Other ....

45   Do you (or your spouse) have another vehicle available for personal use? . . . . ☐ Yes   ☐ No

46   Was your vehicle available for personal use during off-duty hours? . . . . ☐ Yes   ☐ No

47a   Do you have evidence to support your deduction? . . . . ☐ Yes   ☐ No

   b If "Yes," is the evidence written? . . . . ☐ Yes   ☐ No

Part V   **Other Expenses.** List below business expenses not included on lines 8–26 or line 30.

....	
....	
....	
....	
....	
....	
....	
....	
....	
48 **Total other expenses.** Enter here and on page 1, line 27	**48**	

SCHEDULE D
(Form 1040)

Department of the Treasury
Internal Revenue Service   (99)

Capital Gains and Losses

▶ **Attach to Form 1040 or Form 1040NR.**   ▶ **See Instructions for Schedule D (Form 1040).**
▶ **Use Schedule D-1 to list additional transactions for lines 1 and 8.**

OMB No. 1545-0074

2006

Attachment
Sequence No. **12**

Name(s) shown on return

Your social security number

Sch. D

Part I   Short-Term Capital Gains and Losses—Assets Held One Year or Less

(a) Description of property (Example: 100 sh. XYZ Co.)	(b) Date acquired (Mo., day, yr.)	(c) Date sold (Mo., day, yr.)	(d) Sales price (see page D-6 of the instructions)	(e) Cost or other basis (see page D-7 of the instructions)	(f) Gain or (loss) Subtract (e) from (d)
1					

2 Enter your short-term totals, if any, from Schedule D-1, line 2	**2**		
3 **Total short-term sales price amounts.** Add lines 1 and 2 in column (d)	**3**		
4 Short-term gain from Form 6252 and short-term gain or (loss) from Forms 4684, 6781, and 8824	**4**		
5 Net short-term gain or (loss) from partnerships, S corporations, estates, and trusts from Schedule(s) K-1	**5**		
6 Short-term capital loss carryover. Enter the amount, if any, from line 10 of your **Capital Loss Carryover Worksheet** on page D-7 of the instructions	**6** (		)
7 **Net short-term capital gain or (loss).** Combine lines 1 through 6 in column (f)	**7**		

Part II   Long-Term Capital Gains and Losses—Assets Held More Than One Year

(a) Description of property (Example: 100 sh. XYZ Co.)	(b) Date acquired (Mo., day, yr.)	(c) Date sold (Mo., day, yr.)	(d) Sales price (see page D-6 of the instructions)	(e) Cost or other basis (see page D-7 of the instructions)	(f) Gain or (loss) Subtract (e) from (d)
8					

9 Enter your long-term totals, if any, from Schedule D-1, line 9	**9**		
10 **Total long-term sales price amounts.** Add lines 8 and 9 in column (d)	**10**		
11 Gain from Form 4797, Part I; long-term gain from Forms 2439 and 6252; and long-term gain or (loss) from Forms 4684, 6781, and 8824	**11**		
12 Net long-term gain or (loss) from partnerships, S corporations, estates, and trusts from Schedule(s) K-1	**12**		
13 Capital gain distributions. See page D-2 of the instructions	**13**		
14 Long-term capital loss carryover. Enter the amount, if any, from line 15 of your **Capital Loss Carryover Worksheet** on page D-7 of the instructions	**14** (		)
15 **Net long-term capital gain or (loss).** Combine lines 8 through 14 in column (f). Then go to Part III on the back	**15**		

For Paperwork Reduction Act Notice, see Form 1040 or Form 1040NR instructions.   Cat. No. 11338H   **Schedule D (Form 1040) 2006**

Schedule D (Form 1040) 2006   Page **2**

Part III	**Summary**

16   Combine lines 7 and 15 and enter the result. If line 16 is a loss, skip lines 17 through 20, and go to line 21. If a gain, enter the gain on Form 1040, line 13, or Form 1040NR, line 14. Then go to line 17 below **16**

17   Are lines 15 and 16 **both** gains?
   ☐ **Yes.** Go to line 18.
   ☐ **No.** Skip lines 18 through 21, and go to line 22.

18   Enter the amount, if any, from line 7 of the **28% Rate Gain Worksheet** on page D-8 of the instructions . . . . ▶ **18**

19   Enter the amount, if any, from line 18 of the **Unrecaptured Section 1250 Gain Worksheet** on page D-9 of the instructions . . . . ▶ **19**

20   Are lines 18 and 19 **both** zero or blank?
   ☐ **Yes.** Complete Form 1040 through line 43, or Form 1040NR through line 40. Then complete the **Qualified Dividends and Capital Gain Tax Worksheet** on page 38 of the Instructions for Form 1040 (or in the Instructions for Form 1040NR). **Do not** complete lines 21 and 22 below.
   ☐ **No.** Complete Form 1040 through line 43, or Form 1040NR through line 40. Then complete the **Schedule D Tax Worksheet** on page D-10 of the instructions. **Do not** complete lines 21 and 22 below.

21   If line 16 is a loss, enter here and on Form 1040, line 13, or Form 1040NR, line 14, the **smaller** of:

   • The loss on line 16 or
   • ($3,000), or if married filing separately, ($1,500)   . . . . **21** (   )

   Note. When figuring which amount is smaller, treat both amounts as positive numbers.

22   Do you have qualified dividends on Form 1040, line 9b, or Form 1040NR, line 10b?
   ☐ **Yes.** Complete Form 1040 through line 43, or Form 1040NR through line 40. Then complete the **Qualified Dividends and Capital Gain Tax Worksheet** on page 38 of the Instructions for Form 1040 (or in the Instructions for Form 1040NR).
   ☐ **No.** Complete the rest of Form 1040 or Form 1040NR.

Schedule D (Form 1040) 2006

Sch. D

SCHEDULE SE

(Form 1040)

Department of the Treasury
Internal Revenue Service   (99)

Self-Employment Tax

▶ Attach to Form 1040. ▶ See Instructions for Schedule SE (Form 1040).

OMB No. 1545-0074

20**06**

Attachment
Sequence No. **17**

Name of person with **self-employment** income (as shown on Form 1040)	Social security number of person with **self-employment** income ▶

Who Must File Schedule SE

You must file Schedule SE if:

- You had net earnings from self-employment from **other than** church employee income (line 4 of Short Schedule SE or line 4c of Long Schedule SE) of $400 or more, **or**
- You had church employee income of $108.28 or more. Income from services you performed as a minister or a member of a religious order **is not** church employee income (see page SE-1).

Note. Even if you had a loss or a small amount of income from self-employment, it may be to your benefit to file Schedule SE and use either "optional method" in Part II of Long Schedule SE (see page SE-3).

Exception. If your only self-employment income was from earnings as a minister, member of a religious order, or Christian Science practitioner **and** you filed Form 4361 and received IRS approval not to be taxed on those earnings, **do not** file Schedule SE. Instead, write "Exempt–Form 4361" on Form 1040, line 58.

May I Use Short Schedule SE or Must I Use Long Schedule SE?

Note. Use this flowchart **only if** you must file Schedule SE. If unsure, see Who Must File Schedule SE, above.

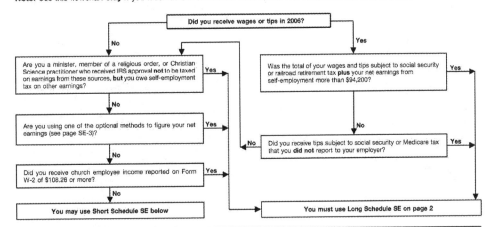

Section A—Short Schedule SE. Caution. Read above to see if you can use Short Schedule SE.

1	Net farm profit or (loss) from Schedule F, line 36, and farm partnerships, Schedule K-1 (Form 1065), box 14, code A	**1**
2	Net profit or (loss) from Schedule C, line 31; Schedule C-EZ, line 3; Schedule K-1 (Form 1065), box 14, code A (other than farming); and Schedule K-1 (Form 1065-B), box 9, code J1. Ministers and members of religious orders, see page SE-1 for amounts to report on this line. See page SE-3 for other income to report	**2**
3	Combine lines 1 and 2	**3**
4	**Net earnings from self-employment.** Multiply line 3 by 92.35% (.9235). If less than $400, **do not** file this schedule; you do not owe self-employment tax . . . . ▶	**4**
5	**Self-employment tax.** If the amount on line 4 is: • $94,200 or less, multiply line 4 by 15.3% (.153). Enter the result here and on **Form 1040, line 58.** • More than $94,200, multiply line 4 by 2.9% (.029). Then, add $11,680.80 to the result. Enter the total here and on **Form 1040, line 58.**	**5**
6	**Deduction for one-half of self-employment tax.** Multiply line 5 by 50% (.5). Enter the result here and on **Form 1040, line 27**	**6**	

For Paperwork Reduction Act Notice, see Form 1040 instructions.   Cat. No. 11358Z   **Schedule SE (Form 1040) 2006**

Form **SS-4**
(Rev. July 2007)
Department of the Treasury
Internal Revenue Service

Application for Employer Identification Number

(For use by employers, corporations, partnerships, trusts, estates, churches, government agencies, Indian tribal entities, certain individuals, and others.)

▶ **See separate instructions for each line.**   ▶ **Keep a copy for your records.**

OMB No 1545-0003

EIN

Type or print clearly.

1 Legal name of entity (or individual) for whom the EIN is being requested	

2 Trade name of business (if different from name on line 1)	**3** Executor, administrator, trustee, "care of" name

4a Mailing address (room, apt., suite no. and street, or P.O. box)	**5a** Street address (if different) (Do not enter a P.O. box.)
4b City, state, and ZIP code (if foreign, see instructions)	**5b** City, state, and ZIP code (if foreign, see instructions)

6 County and state where principal business is located

7a Name of principal officer, general partner, grantor, owner, or trustor	**7b** SSN, ITIN, or EIN

8a Is this application for a limited liability company (LLC) (or a foreign equivalent)? . . . . ☐ **Yes** ☐ **No**

8b If 8a is "Yes," enter the number of LLC members . . . . ▶

8c If 8a is "Yes," was the LLC organized in the United States? . . . . ☐ **Yes** ☐

9a **Type of entity** (check only one box). **Caution.** If 8a is "Yes," see the instructions for the correct box to check.

☐ Sole proprietor (SSN) _____
☐ Partnership
☐ Corporation (enter form number to be filed) ▶ _____
☐ Personal service corporation
☐ Church or church-controlled organization
☐ Other nonprofit organization (specify) ▶ _____
☐ Other (specify) ▶

☐ Estate (SSN of decedent)
☐ Plan administrator (TIN)
☐ Trust (TIN of grantor)
☐ National Guard ☐ State/local government
☐ Farmers' cooperative ☐ Federal government/military
☐ REMIC ☐ Indian tribal governments/enterp
Group Exemption Number (GEN) if any ▶

9b If a corporation, name the state or foreign country (if applicable) where incorporated

State	Foreign country

10 **Reason for applying** (check only one box)

☐ Started new business (specify type) ▶ _____

☐ Hired employees (Check the box and see line 13.)
☐ Compliance with IRS withholding regulations
☐ Other (specify) ▶

☐ Banking purpose (specify purpose) ▶ _____
☐ Changed type of organization (specify new type) ▶ _____
☐ Purchased going business
☐ Created a trust (specify type) ▶ _____
☐ Created a pension plan (specify type) ▶ _____

11 Date business started or acquired (month, day, year). See instructions.

12 Closing month of accounting year

13 Highest number of employees expected in the next 12 months (enter -0- if none).

Agricultural	Household	Other

14 Do you expect your employment tax liability to be $1, or less in a full calendar year? ☐ **Yes** ☐ **No** (If yo expect to pay $4,000 or less in total wages in a full calendar year, you can mark "Yes.")

15 First date wages or annuities were paid (month, day, year). **Note.** If applicant is a withholding agent, enter date income will first be paid nonresident alien (month, day, year) . . . . ▶

16 Check **one** box that best describes the principal activity of your business.
☐ Construction ☐ Rental & leasing ☐ Transportation & warehousing
☐ Real estate ☐ Manufacturing ☐ Finance & insurance
☐ Health care & social assistance ☐ Wholesale-agent/broker
☐ Accommodation & food service ☐ Wholesale-other ☐ R
☐ Other (specify)

17 Indicate principal line of merchandise sold, specific construction work done, products produced, or services provided.

18 Has the applicant entity shown on line 1 ever applied for and received an EIN? ☐ **Yes** ☐ **No**
If "Yes," write previous EIN here ▶

Third Party Designee	Complete this section **only** if you want to authorize the named individual to receive the entity's EIN and answer questions about the completion of this form.	
	Designee's name	Designee's telephone number (include area ( )
	Address and ZIP code	Designee's fax number (include area ( )

Under penalties of perjury, I declare that I have examined this application, and to the best of my knowledge and belief, it is true, correct, and complete.
Name and title (type or print clearly) ▶

Applicant's telephone number (include area ( )

Signature ▶   Date ▶

Applicant's fax number (include area ( )

For Privacy Act and Paperwork Reduction Act Notice, see separate instructions.   Cat. No. 16055N   Form **SS-4** (Rev. 7-

Form W-4 (2007)

Purpose. Complete Form W-4 so that your employer can withhold the correct federal income tax from your pay. Because your tax situation may change, you may want to refigure your withholding each year.

Exemption from withholding. If you are exempt, complete **only** lines 1, 2, 3, 4, and 7 and sign the form to validate it. Your exemption for 2007 expires February 16, 2008. See Pub. 505, Tax Withholding and Estimated Tax.

Note. You cannot claim exemption from withholding if (a) your income exceeds $850 and includes more than $300 of unearned income (for example, interest and dividends) and (b) another person can claim you as a dependent on their tax return.

Basic instructions. If you are not exempt, complete the **Personal Allowances Worksheet** below. The worksheets on page 2 adjust your withholding allowances based on

itemized deductions, certain credits, adjustments to income, or two-earner/multiple job situations. Complete all worksheets that apply. However, you may claim fewer (or zero) allowances.

Head of household. Generally, you may claim head of household filing status on your tax return only if you are unmarried and pay more than 50% of the costs of keeping up a home for yourself and your dependent(s) or other qualifying individuals.

Tax credits. You can take projected tax credits into account in figuring your allowable number of withholding allowances. Credits for child or dependent care expenses and the child tax credit may be claimed using the **Personal Allowances Worksheet** below. See Pub. 919, How Do I Adjust My Tax Withholding, for information on converting your other credits into withholding allowances.

Nonwage income. If you have a large amount of nonwage income, such as interest or dividends, consider making estimated tax payments using Form 1040-ES, Estimated Tax

for Individuals. Otherwise, you may owe additional tax. If you have pension or annuity income, see Pub. 919 to find out if you should adjust your withholding on Form W-4 or W-4P.

Two earners/Multiple jobs. If you have a working spouse or more than one job, figure the total number of allowances you are entitled to claim on all jobs using worksheets from only one Form W-4. Your withholding usually will be most accurate when all allowances are claimed on the Form W-4 for the highest paying job and zero allowances are claimed on the others.

Nonresident alien. If you are a nonresident alien, see the Instructions for Form 8233 before completing this Form W-4.

Check your withholding. After your Form W-4 takes effect, use Pub. 919 to see how the dollar amount you are having withheld compares to your projected total tax for 2007. See Pub. 919, especially if your earnings exceed $130,000 (Single) or $180,000 (Married).

Personal Allowances Worksheet (Keep for your records.)

A Enter "1" for **yourself** if no one else can claim you as a dependent . . . . **A** ___

B Enter "1" if:
- You are single and have only one job; or
- You are married, have only one job, and your spouse does not work; or
- Your wages from a second job or your spouse's wages (or the total of both) are $1,000 or less.

B ___

C Enter "1" for your **spouse.** But, you may choose to enter "-0-" if you are married and have either a working spouse or more than one job. (Entering "-0-" may help you avoid having too little tax withheld.) . . . . **C** ___

D Enter number of **dependents** (other than your spouse or yourself) you will claim on your tax return . . . . . **D** ___

E Enter "1" if you will file as **head of household** on your tax return (see conditions under **Head of household** above) . **E** ___

F Enter "1" if you have at least $1,500 of **child or dependent care expenses** for which you plan to claim a credit . **F** ___
(**Note.** Do **not** include child support payments. See Pub. 503, Child and Dependent Care Expenses, for details.)

G **Child Tax Credit** (including additional child tax credit). See Pub 972, Child Tax Credit, for more information.
- If your total income will be less than $57,000 ($85,000 if married), enter "2" for each eligible child.
- If your total income will be between $57,000 and $84,000 ($85,000 and $119,000 if married), enter "1" for each eligible child plus "1" **additional** if you have 4 or more eligible children. **G** ___

H Add lines A through G and enter total here. (**Note.** This may be different from the number of exemptions you claim on your tax return.) ▶ **H** ___

For accuracy, complete all worksheets that apply.	• If you plan to **itemize or claim adjustments to income** and want to reduce your withholding, see the **Deductions and Adjustments Worksheet** on page 2. • If you have **more than one job** or are **married and you and your spouse both work** and the combined earnings from all jobs exceed $40,000 ($25,000 if married) see the **Two-Earners/Multiple Jobs Worksheet** on page 2 to avoid having too little tax withheld. • If **neither** of the above situations applies, **stop here** and enter the number from line H on line 5 of Form W-4 below.

- - - - - - - - - - - - - - - **Cut here and give Form W-4 to your employer. Keep the top part for your records.** - - - - - - - - - - - - - - -

Form **W-4**

Department of the Treasury
Internal Revenue Service

Employee's Withholding Allowance Certificate

▶ **Whether you are entitled to claim a certain number of allowances or exemption from withholding is subject to review by the IRS. Your employer may be required to send a copy of this form to the IRS.**

OMB No. 1545-0074

2007

1 Type or print your first name and middle initial.	Last name	2 Your social security number

Home address (number and street or rural route)	3 ☐ Single ☐ Married ☐ Married. but withhold at higher Single rate. **Note.** If married, but legally separated, or spouse is a nonresident alien, check the "Single" box.
City or town, state, and ZIP code	4 If your last name differs from that shown on your social security card, check here. You must call 1-800-772-1213 for a replacement card. ▶ ☐

5 Total number of allowances you are claiming (from line **H** above **or** from the applicable worksheet on page 2) — **5** ___

6 Additional amount, if any, you want withheld from each paycheck — **6** $ ___

7 I claim exemption from withholding for 2007, and I certify that I meet **both** of the following conditions for exemption.
- Last year I had a right to a refund of **all** federal income tax withheld because I had **no** tax liability **and**
- This year I expect a refund of **all** federal income tax withheld because I expect to have **no** tax liability.

If you meet both conditions, write "Exempt" here . . . . ▶ **7** ___

Under penalties of perjury, I declare that I have examined this certificate and to the best of my knowledge and belief, it is true, correct, and complete.

Employee's signature
(Form is not valid
unless you sign it.) ▶ _____ Date ▶ _____

8 Employer's name and address (Employer: Complete lines 8 and 10 only if sending to the IRS.)	9 Office code (optional)	10 Employer identification number (EIN)

For Privacy Act and Paperwork Reduction Act Notice, see page 2. Cat. No. 10220Q Form **W-4** (2007)

Form **940 for 2006:** Employer's Annual Federal Unemployment (FUTA) Tax Return   850106

Department of the Treasury — Internal Revenue Service

OMB No. 1545-0028

(EIN)
Employer identification number   ☐ ☐ ☐ — ☐ ☐ ☐ ☐ ☐ ☐ ☐

Name *(not your trade name)*

Trade name *(if any)*

Address
Number   Street   Suite or room number
City   State   ZIP code

Type of Return
(Check all that apply.)

☐ **a.** Amended
☐ **b.** Successor employer
☐ **c.** No payments to employees in 2006
☐ **d.** Final: Business closed or stopped paying wages

Read the separate instructions before you fill out this form. Please type or print within the boxes.

Part 1: Tell us about your return. If any line does NOT apply, leave it blank.

1   If you were required to pay your state unemployment tax in ...

   1a One state only, write the state abbreviation . . . . . **1a** ☐ ☐
   - OR -
   1b More than one state (You are a multi-state employer) . . . . **1b** ☐ Check here. Fill out Schedule A.

2

Part 2: Determine your FUTA tax before adjustments for 2006. If any line does NOT apply, leave it blank.

3   Total payments to all employees . . . . **3** [   ]

4   Payments exempt from FUTA tax . . . . **4** [   ]

   Check all that apply: **4a** ☐ Fringe benefits   **4c** ☐ Retirement/Pension   **4e** ☐ Other
   4b ☐ Group term life insurance   **4d** ☐ Dependent care

5   Total of payments made to each employee in excess of $7,000 . . . . . **5** [   ]

6   Subtotal (line 4 + line 5 = line 6) . . . . . . **6** [   ]

7   Total taxable FUTA wages (line 3 – line 6 = line 7) . . . . **7** [   ]

8   FUTA tax before adjustments (line 7 × .008 = line 8) . . . . **8** [   ]

Part 3: Determine your adjustments. If any line does NOT apply, leave it blank.

9   If ALL of the taxable FUTA wages you paid were excluded from state unemployment tax, multiply line 7 by .054 (line 7 × .054 = line 9). Then go to line 12 . . . . **9** [   ]

10   If SOME of the taxable FUTA wages you paid were excluded from state unemployment tax, OR you paid ANY state unemployment tax late (after the due date for filing Form 940), fill out the worksheet in the instructions. Enter the amount from line 7 of the worksheet onto line 10 . . **10** [   ]

11

Part 4: Determine your FUTA tax and balance due or overpayment for 2006. If any line does NOT apply, leave it blank.

12   Total FUTA tax after adjustments (lines 8 + 9 + 10 = line 12) . . . . **12** [   ]

13   FUTA tax deposited for the year, including any payment applied from a prior year . . . . **13** [   ]

14   Balance due (If line 12 is more than line 13, enter the difference on line 14.)
   • If line 14 is more than $500, you must deposit your tax.
   • If line 14 is $500 or less and you pay by check, make your check payable to the United States Treasury and write your EIN, *Form 940*, and *2006* on the check . . . . **14** [   ]

15   Overpayment (If line 13 is more than line 12, enter the difference on line 15 and check a box below.) . . . . **15** [   ]

   Check one ☐ Apply to next return.
   ☐ Send a refund.

▶ You **MUST** fill out both pages of this form and **SIGN** it.

Next ➡

For Privacy Act and Paperwork Reduction Act Notice, see the back of Form 940-V, Payment Voucher.   Cat. No. 11234O   Form **940** (2006)

850206

Name *(not your trade name)*	Employer identification number (EIN)

Part 5: Report your FUTA tax liability by quarter only if line 12 is more than $500. If not, go to Part 6.

16 Report the amount of your FUTA tax liability for each quarter; do **NOT** enter the amount you deposited. If you had no liability for a quarter, leave the line blank.

16a **1st quarter** (January 1 – March 31) . . . . **16a** [.   ]

16b **2nd quarter** (April 1 – June 30) . . . . **16b** [.   ]

16c **3rd quarter** (July 1 – September 30) . . . . **16c** [.   ]

16d **4th quarter** (October 1 – December 31) . . . . **16d** [.   ]

17 Total tax liability for the year (lines 16a + 16b + 16c + 16d = line 17) **17** [.   ] Total must equal line 12.

Part 6: May we speak with your third-party designee?

Do you want to allow an employee, a paid tax preparer, or another person to discuss this return with the IRS? See the instructions for details.

☐ **Yes.** Designee's name [   ]

Select a 5-digit Personal Identification Number (PIN) to use when talking to IRS [ ] [ ] [ ] [ ] [ ]

☐ **No.**

Part 7: Sign here.

You MUST fill out both pages of this form and SIGN it.

Under penalties of perjury, I declare that I have examined this return, including accompanying schedules and statements, and to the best of my knowledge and belief, it is true, correct, and complete, and that no part of any payment made to a state unemployment fund claimed as a credit was, or is to be, deducted from the payments made to employees.

✗ **Sign your name here** [   ]   Print your name here [   ]

Print your title here [   ]

Date [/   /   ]   Best daytime phone [(   )   –   ]

Part 8: For PAID preparers only (optional)

If you were paid to prepare this return and are not an employee of the business that is filing this return, you may choose to fill out Part 8.

Paid Preparer's name [   ]   Preparer's SSN/PTIN [   ]

Paid Preparer's signature [   ]   Date [/   /   ]

☐ Check if you are self-employed.

Firm's name [   ]   Firm's EIN [   ]

Street address [   ]

City [   ]   State [   ]   ZIP code [   ]

940

Form 941 for 2007: **Employer's QUARTERLY Federal Tax Return**

990107

(Rev. January 2007)

Department of the Treasury — Internal Revenue Service

OMB No. 1545-0029

(EIN)
Employer identification number ☐☐ — ☐☐☐☐☐☐☐

Name (not your trade name)

Trade name (if any)

Address
Number   Street   Suite or room number
City   State   ZIP code

Report for this Quarter of 2007
(Check one.)

☐ **1:** January, February, March

☐ **2:** April, May, June

☐ **3:** July, August, September

☐ **4:** October, November, December

Read the separate instructions before you fill out this form. Please type or print within the boxes.

Part 1: Answer these questions for this quarter.

1 Number of employees who received wages, tips, or other compensation for the pay period including: *Mar. 12 (Quarter 1), June 12 (Quarter 2), Sept. 12 (Quarter 3), Dec. 12 (Quarter 4)*   1

2 Wages, tips, and other compensation   2

3 Total income tax withheld from wages, tips, and other compensation   3

4 If no wages, tips, and other compensation are subject to social security or Medicare tax . . ☐ Check and go to line 6.

5 Taxable social security and Medicare wages and tips:

	Column 1		Column 2
5a Taxable social security wages		× .124 =	
5b Taxable social security tips		× .124 =	
5c Taxable Medicare wages & tips		× .029 =	

5d Total social security and Medicare taxes (*Column 2*, lines 5a + 5b + 5c = line 5d) .   5d

6 Total taxes before adjustments (lines 3 + 5d = line 6)   6

7 TAX ADJUSTMENTS (Read the instructions for line 7 before completing lines 7a through 7h.):

7a Current quarter's fractions of cents . . . .

7b Current quarter's sick pay . . . .

7c Current quarter's adjustments for tips and group-term life insurance

7d Current year's income tax withholding (attach Form 941c) . .

7e Prior quarters' social security and Medicare taxes (attach Form 941c)

7f Special additions to federal income tax (attach Form 941c) . .

7g Special additions to social security and Medicare (attach Form 941c)

7h TOTAL ADJUSTMENTS (Combine all amounts: lines 7a through 7g.) 7h

8 Total taxes after adjustments (Combine lines 6 and 7h.)   8

9 Advance earned income credit (EIC) payments made to employees   9

10 Total taxes after adjustment for advance EIC (line 8 – line 9 = line 10)   10

11 Total deposits for this quarter, including overpayment applied from a prior quarter . . .   11

12 Balance due (If line 10 is more than line 11, write the difference here.)   12
Follow the Instructions for Form 941-V, Payment Voucher.

13 Overpayment (If line 11 is more than line 10, write the difference here.)   Check one ☐ Apply to next return.
☐ Send a refund.

▶ You **MUST** fill out both pages of this form and **SIGN** it.

Next ➡

For Privacy Act and Paperwork Reduction Act Notice, see the back of the Payment Voucher.   Cat. No. 17001Z   Form **941** (Rev. 1-2007)

990207

Name *(not your trade name)*	Employer identification number (EIN)

Part 2: Tell us about your deposit schedule and tax liability for this quarter.

If you are unsure about whether you are a monthly schedule depositor or a semiweekly schedule depositor, see *Pub. 15 (Circular E),* section 11.

14 ☐ ☐ Write the state abbreviation for the state where you made your deposits OR write "MU" if you made your deposits in *multiple* states.

15 Check one: ☐ Line 10 is less than $2,500. Go to Part 3.

☐ You were a monthly schedule depositor for the entire quarter. Fill out your tax liability for each month. Then go to Part 3.

Tax liability: Month 1 [_____.__]

Month 2 [_____.__]

Month 3 [_____.__]

Total liability for quarter [_____.__] Total must equal line 10.

☐ You were a semiweekly schedule depositor for any part of this quarter. Fill out *Schedule B (Form 941): Report of Tax Liability for Semiweekly Schedule Depositors,* and attach it to this form.

Part 3: Tell us about your business. If a question does NOT apply to your business, leave it blank.

16 If your business has closed or you stopped paying wages . . . . ☐ Check here, and

enter the final date you paid wages [__/__/__]

17 If you are a seasonal employer and you do not have to file a return for every quarter of the year . . ☐ Check here.

Part 4: May we speak with your third-party designee?

Do you want to allow an employee, a paid tax preparer, or another person to discuss this return with the IRS? (See the instructions for details.)

☐ Yes. Designee's name [_____]

Select a 5-digit Personal Identification Number (PIN) to use when talking to IRS. ☐ ☐ ☐ ☐ ☐

☐ No.

Part 5: Sign here. You MUST fill out both pages of this form and SIGN it.

Under penalties of perjury, I declare that I have examined this return, including accompanying schedules and statements, and to the best of my knowledge and belief, it is true, correct, and complete.

X Sign your name here [_____]

Print your name here [_____]

Print your title here [_____]

Date [__/__/__]

Best daytime phone ( ) –

Part 6: For paid preparers only *(optional)*

Paid Preparer's Signature			
Firm's name			
Address		EIN	
		ZIP code	
Date [__/__/__] Phone ( ) –		SSN/PTIN	
☐ Check if you are self-employed.			

Form **941** (Rev. 1-2007)

941

Form **944 for 2006:** **Employer's ANNUAL Federal Tax Return**   790106

Department of the Treasury — Internal Revenue Service

OMB No. 1545-2007

Employer identification number (EIN) [ ][ ] – [ ][ ][ ][ ][ ][ ]

Name *(not your trade name)*

Trade name *(if any)*

Address

Number   Street   Suite or room number

City   State   ZIP code

Read the separate instructions before you fill out this form. Please type or print within the boxes.

Part 1: Answer these questions for 2006.

1 Wages, tips, and other compensation . . . .   **1** [   ] .

2 Total income tax withheld from wages, tips, and other compensation . . . . . .   **2** [   ] .

3 If no wages, tips, and other compensation are subject to social security or Medicare tax .   **3** ☐ Check and go to line 5.

4 Taxable social security and Medicare wages and tips:

	Column 1		Column 2
4a Taxable social security wages	[ ] .	× .124 =	[ ] .
4b Taxable social security tips	[ ] .	× .124 =	[ ] .
4c Taxable Medicare wages & tips	[ ] .	× .029 =	[ ] .

4d Total social security and Medicare taxes (*Column 2*, lines 4a + 4b + 4c = line 4d) . . .   **4d** [   ] .

5 Total taxes before adjustments (lines 2 + 4d = line 5) . . . .   **5** [   ] .

6 **TAX ADJUSTMENTS** (Read the instructions for line 6 before completing lines 6a through 6f.):

6a Current year's adjustments (See instructions) . . . . . .   **6a** [   ] .

6b Prior years' income tax withholding adjustments (See instructions. Attach Form 941c.) . . . .   **6b** [   ] .

6c Prior years' social security and Medicare tax adjustments (See instructions. Attach Form 941c.) . . . . . .   **6c** [   ] .

6d Special additions to federal income tax (reserved use). Attach Form 941c . . . .   **6d** [   ] .

6e Special additions to social security and Medicare taxes (reserved use). Attach Form 941c . . . .   **6e** [   ] .

6f **TOTAL ADJUSTMENTS** (Combine all amounts: lines 6a through 6e.) . . . .   **6f** [   ] .

7 Total taxes after adjustments (Combine lines 5 and 6f.) . . . .   **7** [   ] .

8 Advance earned income credit (EIC) payments made to employees . . . .   **8** [   ] .

9 Total taxes after adjustment for advance EIC (line 7 – line 8 = line 9) . . . .   **9** [   ] .

10 Total deposits for this year, including overpayment applied from a prior year . . .   **10** [   ] .

11 **Balance due** (If line 9 is more than line 10, write the difference here.) Make your check payable to the *United States Treasury* and write your EIN, *Form 944*, and *2006* on the check . . . . .   **11** [   ] .

12 **Overpayment** (If line 10 is more than line 9, write the difference here.)   **12** [   ] .   Check one ☐ Apply to next return.   ☐ Send a refund.

▶ You MUST fill out both pages of this form and SIGN it.

Next ➡

For Privacy Act and Paperwork Reduction Act Notice, see the back of the Payment Voucher.   Cat. No. 39316N   Form **944** (2006)

790206

Name *(not your trade name)*	Employer identification number (EIN)

Part 2: Tell us about your tax liability for 2006.

13 Check one: ☐ Line 9 is less than $2,500. Go to Part 3.

☐ Line 9 is $2,500 or more, fill out your tax liability for each month.

	Jan.		Apr.		Jul.		Oct.
13a		13d		13g		13j	
	Feb.		May		Aug.		Nov.
13b		13e		13h		13k	
	Mar.		Jun.		Sep.		Dec.
13c		13f		13i		13l	

Total liability for year (Add lines 13a through 13l). Total must equal line 9. 13m

14 ☐☐ If you made deposits of taxes reported on this form, write the state abbreviation for the state where you made your deposits OR write *MU* if you made your deposits in *multiple* states.

Part 3: Tell us about your business. If question 15 does NOT apply to your business, leave it blank.

15 If your business has closed or you stopped paying wages...

☐ Check here and enter the final date you paid wages.   /   /

Part 4: May we speak with your third-party designee?

Do you want to allow an employee, a paid tax preparer, or another person to discuss this return with the IRS? (See the instructions for details.)

☐ Yes. Designee's name

Select a 5-digit Personal Identification Number (PIN) to use when talking to IRS. ☐☐☐☐☐

☐ No.

Part 5: Sign here. You MUST fill out both pages of this form and SIGN it.

Under penalties of perjury, I declare that I have examined this return, including accompanying schedules and statements, and to the best of my knowledge and belief, it is true, correct, and complete.

X Sign your name here

Print your name here

Print your title here

Date   /   /

Best daytime phone (   )   —

Part 6: For paid preparers only *(optional)*

If you were PAID to prepare this return and are not an employee of the business that is filing this return, you may choose to fill out Part 6.

Paid Preparer's name

Preparer's SSN/PTIN

Paid Preparer's signature

Date   /   /

☐ Check if you are self employed.

Firm's name

Firm's EIN

Address

City

State

ZIP code

Page **2**

Form **944** (2006)

944

Form 1040-ES
Department of the Treasury
Internal Revenue Service

2007 Payment Voucher **3**

OMB No. 1545-0074

File only if you are making a payment of estimated tax by check or money order. Mail this voucher with your check or money order payable to the **"United States Treasury."** Write your social security number and "2007 Form 1040-ES" on your check or money order. Do not send cash. Enclose, but do not staple or attach, your payment with this voucher.

Calendar year—Due Sept. 17, 2007

Amount of estimated tax you are paying by check or money order.

	Dollars	Cents

Print or type

Your first name and initial	Your last name	Your social security number

If joint payment, complete for spouse

Spouse's first name and initial	Spouse's last name	Spouse's social security number

Address (number, street, and apt. no.)

City, state, and ZIP code. (If a foreign address, enter city, province or state, postal code, and country.)

For Privacy Act and Paperwork Reduction Act Notice, see instructions on page 5.

------------------------------ **Tear off here** ------------------------------

Form 1040-ES
Department of the Treasury
Internal Revenue Service

2007 Payment Voucher **2**

OMB No. 1545-0074

File only if you are making a payment of estimated tax by check or money order. Mail this voucher with your check or money order payable to the **"United States Treasury."** Write your social security number and "2007 Form 1040-ES" on your check or money order. Do not send cash. Enclose, but do not staple or attach, your payment with this voucher.

Calendar year—Due June 15, 2007

Amount of estimated tax you are paying by check or money order.

	Dollars	Cents

Print or type

Your first name and initial	Your last name	Your social security number

If joint payment, complete for spouse

Spouse's first name and initial	Spouse's last name	Spouse's social security number

Address (number, street, and apt. no.)

City, state, and ZIP code. (If a foreign address, enter city, province or state, postal code, and country.)

For Privacy Act and Paperwork Reduction Act Notice, see instructions on page 5.

------------------------------ **Tear off here** ------------------------------

Form 1040-ES
Department of the Treasury
Internal Revenue Service

2007 Payment Voucher **1**

OMB No. 1545-0074

File only if you are making a payment of estimated tax by check or money order. Mail this voucher with your check or money order payable to the **"United States Treasury."** Write your social security number and "2007 Form 1040-ES" on your check or money order. Do not send cash. Enclose, but do not staple or attach, your payment with this voucher.

Calendar year—Due April 16, 2007

Amount of estimated tax you are paying by check or money order.

	Dollars	Cents

Print or type

Your first name and initial	Your last name	Your social security number

If joint payment, complete for spouse

Spouse's first name and initial	Spouse's last name	Spouse's social security number

Address (number, street, and apt. no.)

City, state, and ZIP code. (If a foreign address, enter city, province or state, postal code, and country.)

For Privacy Act and Paperwork Reduction Act Notice, see instructions on page 5.

Page 7

Form 1040X
(Rev. February 2007)

Department of the Treasury—Internal Revenue Service

Amended U.S. Individual Income Tax Return
▶ See separate instructions.

OMB No. 1545-0074

This return is for calendar year ▶ _____ , or fiscal year ended ▶ _____

Please print or type

Your first name and initial	Last name	Your social security number
If a joint return, spouse's first name and initial	Last name	Spouse's social security number
Home address (no. and street) or P.O. box if mail is not delivered to your home	Apt. no.	Phone number ( )
City, town or post office, state, and ZIP code. If you have a foreign address, see page 3 of the instructions.		

A If the address shown above is different from that shown on your last return filed with the IRS, would you like us to change it in our records? . . . . ▶ ☐ Yes ☐ No

B Filing status. Be sure to complete this line. **Note.** You cannot change from joint to separate returns after the due date.

On original return ▶ ☐ Single ☐ Married filing jointly ☐ Married filing separately ☐ Head of household ☐ Qualifying widow(er)

On this return ▶ ☐ Single ☐ Married filing jointly ☐ Married filing separately ☐ Head of household* ☐ Qualifying widow(er)

* If the qualifying person is a child but not your dependent, see page 3 of the instructions.

Use Part II on the back to explain any changes

				A. Original amount or as previously adjusted (see page 3)	B. Net change—amount of increase or (decrease)—explain in Part II	C. Correct amount
Income and Deductions (see instructions)						
1	Adjusted gross income (see page 3)	**1**				
2	Itemized deductions or standard deduction (see page 3) .	**2**				
3	Subtract line 2 from line 1	**3**				
4	Exemptions. If changing, fill in Parts I and II on the back (see page 4)	**4**				
5	Taxable income. Subtract line 4 from line 3	**5**				
6	Tax (see page 5). Method used in col. C_____	**6**				
7	Credits (see page 5)	**7**				
8	Subtract line 7 from line 6. Enter the result but not less than zero	**8**				
9	Other taxes (see page 5)	**9**				
10	Total tax. Add lines 8 and 9	**10**				
11	Federal income tax withheld and excess social security and tier 1 RRTA tax withheld. If changing, see page 5 . . .	**11**				
12	Estimated tax payments, including amount applied from prior year's return	**12**				
13	Earned income credit (EIC)	**13**				
14	Additional child tax credit from Form 8812	**14**				
15	Credits: Federal telephone excise tax or from Forms 2439, 4136, or 8885	**15**				
16	Amount paid with request for extension of time to file (see page 5)				**16**	
17	Amount of tax paid with original return plus additional tax paid after it was filed				**17**	
18	Total payments. Add lines 11 through 17 in column C				**18**	
Refund or Amount You Owe						
19	Overpayment, if any, as shown on original return or as previously adjusted by the IRS . . .				**19**	
20	Subtract line 19 from line 18 (see page 6)				**20**	
21	**Amount you owe.** If line 10, column C, is more than line 20, enter the difference and see page 6 .				**21**	
22	If line 10, column C, is less than line 20, enter the difference				**22**	
23	Amount of line 22 you want **refunded to you**				**23**	
24	Amount of line 22 you want **applied to your** estimated tax ▶ **24**					

Tax Liability (lines 6–10) | Payments (lines 11–18)

Sign Here

Joint return? See page 2. Keep a copy for your records.

Under penalties of perjury, I declare that I have filed an original return and that I have examined this amended return, including accompanying schedules and statements, and to the best of my knowledge and belief, this amended return is true, correct, and complete. Declaration of preparer (other than taxpayer) is based on all information of which the preparer has any knowledge.

| ▶ Your signature | Date | ▶ Spouse's signature. If a joint return, **both must sign.** | Date |

Paid Preparer's Use Only

Preparer's signature ▶	Date	Check if self-employed ☐	Preparer's SSN or PTIN
Firm's name (or yours if self-employed), address, and ZIP code ▶		EIN	
		Phone no. ( )	

For Paperwork Reduction Act Notice, see page 6 of instructions.　Cat. No. 11360L　Form **1040X** (Rev. 2-2007)

1040ES

3115

Form 3115
(Rev. December 2003)
Department of the Treasury
Internal Revenue Service

Application for Change in Accounting Method

OMB No. 1545-0152

Name of filer (name of parent corporation if a consolidated group) (see instructions)	Identification number (see instructions)
	Principal business activity code number (see instructions)
Number, street, and room or suite no. If a P.O. box, see the instructions.	Tax year of change begins (MM/DD/YYYY)
	Tax year of change ends (MM/DD/YYYY)
City or town, state, and ZIP code	Name of contact person (see instructions)
Name of applicant(s) (if different than filer) and identification number(s) (see instructions)	Contact person's telephone number ( )

If the applicant is a member of a consolidated group, check this box . . . . ▶ ☐

If **Form 2848,** Power of Attorney and Declaration of Representative, is attached, check this box . . . . . ▶ ☐

Check the box to indicate the applicant.

☐ Individual
☐ Corporation
☐ Controlled foreign corporation (Sec. 957)
☐ 10/50 corporation (Sec. 904(d)(2)(E))
☐ Qualified personal service corporation (Sec. 448(d)(2))
☐ Exempt organization. Enter Code section ▶ ....

☐ Cooperative (Sec. 1381)
☐ Partnership
☐ S corporation
☐ Insurance co. (Sec. 816(a))
☐ Insurance co. (Sec. 831)
☐ Other (specify) ▶ ....

Check the appropriate box to indicate the type of accounting method change being requested. (see instructions)

☐ Depreciation or Amortization
☐ Financial Products and/or Financial Activities of Financial Institutions
☐ Other (specify) ▶ ....

Caution: *The applicant must provide the requested information to be eligible for approval of the requested accounting method change. The applicant may be required to provide information specific to the accounting method change such as an attached statement. The applicant must provide all information relevant to the requested accounting method change, even if not specifically requested by the Form 3115.*

Part I	**Information For Automatic Change Request**	Yes	No
1	Enter the requested designated accounting method change number from the **List of Automatic Accounting Method Changes** (see instructions). Enter only one method change number, except as provided for in the instructions. If the requested change is not included in that list, check "Other," and provide a description.		
	▶ (a) Change No. _____ (b) Other ☐ Description ▶ _____		
2	Is the accounting method change being requested one for which the scope limitations of section 4.02 of Rev. Proc. 2002-9 (or its successor) **do not** apply?		
	If "Yes," go to Part II.		
3	Is the tax year of change the final tax year of a trade or business for which the taxpayer would be required to take the entire amount of the section 481(a) adjustment into account in computing taxable income? . . .		
	If "Yes," the applicant is not eligible to make the change under automatic change request procedures.		

Note: *Complete Part II below and then Part IV, and also Schedules A through E of this form (if applicable).*

Part II	**Information For All Requests**	Yes	No
4a	Does the applicant (or any present or former consolidated group in which the applicant was a member during the applicable tax year(s)) have any Federal income tax return(s) under examination (see instructions)? . . .		
	If you answered "No," go to line 5.		
b	Is the method of accounting the applicant is requesting to change an issue (with respect to either the applicant or any present or former consolidated group in which the applicant was a member during the applicable tax year(s)) either (i) under consideration or (ii) placed in suspense (see instructions)?		

Signature *(see instructions)*

Under penalties of perjury, I declare that I have examined this application, including accompanying schedules and statements, and to the best of my knowledge and belief, the application contains all the relevant facts relating to the application, and it is true, correct, and complete. Declaration of preparer (other than applicant) is based on all information of which preparer has any knowledge.

Filer	**Preparer (other than filer/applicant)**
Signature and date	Signature of individual preparing the application and date
Name and title (print or type)	Name of individual preparing the application (print or type)
	Name of firm preparing the application

For Privacy Act and Paperwork Reduction Act Notice, see the instructions.   Cat. No. 19280E   Form **3115** (Rev. 12-2003)

Form **4562**	**Depreciation and Amortization**	OMB No. 1545-0172

Form 4562

Department of the Treasury
Internal Revenue Service

Depreciation and Amortization

(Including Information on Listed Property)

▶ **See separate instructions.** ▶ **Attach to your tax return.**

OMB No. 1545-0172

2006

Attachment
Sequence No. **67**

Name(s) shown on return	Business or activity to which this form relates	Identifying number

4562

Part I — Election To Expense Certain Property Under Section 179
Note: *If you have any listed property, complete Part V before you complete Part I.*

1	Maximum amount. See the instructions for a higher limit for certain businesses	1	$108,000
2	Total cost of section 179 property placed in service (see instructions)	2	
3	Threshold cost of section 179 property before reduction in limitation	3	$430,000
4	Reduction in limitation. Subtract line 3 from line 2. If zero or less, enter -0-	4	
5	Dollar limitation for tax year. Subtract line 4 from line 1. If zero or less, enter -0-. If married filing separately, see instructions	5	

(a) Description of property	(b) Cost (business use only)	(c) Elected cost
6		

7	Listed property. Enter the amount from line 29 . . . . **7**		
8	Total elected cost of section 179 property. Add amounts in column (c), lines 6 and 7	8	
9	Tentative deduction. Enter the **smaller** of line 5 or line 8	9	
10	Carryover of disallowed deduction from line 13 of your 2005 Form 4562	10	
11	Business income limitation. Enter the smaller of business income (not less than zero) or line 5 (see instructions)	11	
12	Section 179 expense deduction. Add lines 9 and 10, but do not enter more than line 11	12	
13	Carryover of disallowed deduction to 2007. Add lines 9 and 10, less line 12 ▶ **13**		

Note: *Do not use Part II or Part III below for listed property. Instead, use Part V.*

Part II — Special Depreciation Allowance and Other Depreciation (Do not include listed property.) (See instructions.)

14	Special allowance for qualified New York Liberty or Gulf Opportunity Zone property (other than listed property) placed in service during the tax year (see instructions)	14	
15	Property subject to section 168(f)(1) election	15	
16	Other depreciation (including ACRS)	16	

Part III — MACRS Depreciation (Do not include listed property.) (See instructions.)

Section A

17	MACRS deductions for assets placed in service in tax years beginning before 2006	17	
18	If you are electing to group any assets placed in service during the tax year into one or more general asset accounts, check here . . . . ▶ ☐		

Section B—Assets Placed in Service During 2006 Tax Year Using the General Depreciation System

(a) Classification of property	(b) Month and year placed in service	(c) Basis for depreciation (business/investment use only—see instructions)	(d) Recovery period	(e) Convention	(f) Method	(g) Depreciation deduction
19a 3-year property						
b 5-year property						
c 7-year property						
d 10-year property						
e 15-year property						
f 20-year property						
g 25-year property			25 yrs.		S/L	
h Residential rental property			27.5 yrs.	MM	S/L	
			27.5 yrs.	MM	S/L	
i Nonresidential real property			39 yrs.	MM	S/L	
				MM	S/L	

Section C—Assets Placed in Service During 2006 Tax Year Using the Alternative Depreciation System

20a Class life					S/L	
b 12-year			12 yrs.		S/L	
c 40-year			40 yrs.	MM	S/L	

Part IV — Summary (see instructions)

21	Listed property. Enter amount from line 28	21	
22	**Total.** Add amounts from line 12, lines 14 through 17, lines 19 and 20 in column (g), and line 21. Enter here and on the appropriate lines of your return. Partnerships and S corporations—see instr.	22	
23	For assets shown above and placed in service during the current year, enter the portion of the basis attributable to section 263A costs . . **23**		

For Paperwork Reduction Act Notice, see separate instructions. Cat. No. 12906N Form **4562** (2006)

Form 4562 (2006)   Page **2**

Part V   **Listed Property** (Include automobiles, certain other vehicles, cellular telephones, certain computers, and property used for entertainment, recreation, or amusement.)

Note: *For any vehicle for which you are using the standard mileage rate or deducting lease expense, complete only 24a, 24b, columns (a) through (c) of Section A, all of Section B, and Section C if applicable.*

Section A—Depreciation and Other Information (Caution: *See the instructions for limits for passenger automobiles.***)**

| 24a Do you have evidence to support the business/investment use claimed? ☐ Yes ☐ No | | | | | 24b If "Yes," is the evidence written? ☐ Yes ☐ No | | | | |

(a) Type of property (list vehicles first)	(b) Date placed in service	(c) Business/investment use percentage	(d) Cost or other basis	(e) Basis for depreciation (business/investment use only)	(f) Recovery period	(g) Method/ Convention	(h) Depreciation deduction	(i) Elected section 179 cost
25 Special allowance for qualified New York Liberty or Gulf Opportunity Zone property placed in service during the tax year and used more than 50% in a qualified business use (see instructions) **25**								
26 Property used more than 50% in a qualified business use:								
		%						
		%						
		%						
27 Property used 50% or less in a qualified business use:								
		%					S/L –	
		%					S/L –	
		%					S/L –	
28 Add amounts in column (h), lines 25 through 27. Enter here and on line 21, page 1 . . **28**								
29 Add amounts in column (i), line 26. Enter here and on line 7, page 1 . . . . **29**								

Section B—Information on Use of Vehicles

Complete this section for vehicles used by a sole proprietor, partner, or other "more than 5% owner," or related person.

If you provided vehicles to your employees, first answer the questions in Section C to see if you meet an exception to completing this section for those vehicles.

		(a) Vehicle 1		(b) Vehicle 2		(c) Vehicle 3		(d) Vehicle 4		(e) Vehicle 5		(f) Vehicle 6	
30	Total business/investment miles driven during the year (**do not** include commuting miles)												
31	Total commuting miles driven during the year												
32	Total other personal (noncommuting) miles driven												
33	Total miles driven during the year. Add lines 30 through 32												
34	Was the vehicle available for personal use during off-duty hours?	Yes	No	Yes	No	Yes	No	Yes	No	Yes	No	Yes	No
35	Was the vehicle used primarily by a more than 5% owner or related person?												
36	Is another vehicle available for personal use?												

Section C—Questions for Employers Who Provide Vehicles for Use by Their Employees

Answer these questions to determine if you meet an exception to completing Section B for vehicles used by employees who **are not** more than 5% owners or related persons (see instructions).

		Yes	No
37	Do you maintain a written policy statement that prohibits all personal use of vehicles, including commuting, by your employees?		
38	Do you maintain a written policy statement that prohibits personal use of vehicles, except commuting, by your employees? See the instructions for vehicles used by corporate officers, directors, or 1% or more owners		
39	Do you treat all use of vehicles by employees as personal use?		
40	Do you provide more than five vehicles to your employees, obtain information from your employees about the use of the vehicles, and retain the information received?		
41	Do you meet the requirements concerning qualified automobile demonstration use? (See instructions.)		

Note: *If your answer to 37, 38, 39, 40, or 41 is "Yes," do not complete Section B for the covered vehicles.*

Part VI   **Amortization**

(a) Description of costs	(b) Date amortization begins	(c) Amortizable amount	(d) Code section	(e) Amortization period or percentage	(f) Amortization for this year
42 Amortization of costs that begins during your 2006 tax year (see instructions):					
43 Amortization of costs that began before your 2006 tax year **43**					
44 **Total.** Add amounts in column (f). See the instructions for where to report **44**					

Form **4562** (2006)

Form **4684**

Department of the Treasury
Internal Revenue Service

Casualties and Thefts

▶ **See separate instructions.**
▶ **Attach to your tax return.**
▶ **Use a separate Form 4684 for each casualty or theft.**

OMB No. 1545-0177

2006

Attachment
Sequence No. **26**

Name(s) shown on tax return

Identifying number

SECTION A—Personal Use Property (Use this section to report casualties and thefts of property **not** used in a trade or business or for income-producing purposes.)

1 Description of properties (show type, location, and date acquired for each property). Use a separate line for each property lost or damaged from the same casualty or theft.

Property **A**
Property **B**
Property **C**
Property **D**

		Properties		
	A	B	C	D
2 Cost or other basis of each property				
3 Insurance or other reimbursement (whether or not you filed a claim) (see instructions)				
Note: *If line 2 is more than line 3, skip line 4.*				
4 Gain from casualty or theft. If line 3 is **more** than line 2, enter the difference here and skip lines 5 through 9 for that column. See instructions if line 3 includes insurance or other reimbursement you did not claim, or you received payment for your loss in a later tax year				
5 Fair market value **before** casualty or theft				
6 Fair market value **after** casualty or theft				
7 Subtract line 6 from line 5				
8 Enter the **smaller** of line 2 or line 7				
9 Subtract line 3 from line 8. If zero or less, enter -0-				

10 Casualty or theft loss. Add the amounts on line 9 in columns A through D · · · · · · · · | **10** |

11 Enter the **smaller** of line 10 or $100. But if the loss arose in the Hurricane Katrina disaster area after August 24, 2005; Hurricane Rita disaster area after September 22, 2005; or Hurricane Wilma disaster area after October 22, 2005, and was caused by that particular hurricane, enter -0- · · · · · · · · · | **11** |

12 Subtract line 11 from line 10 · · · · · · · | **12** |

Caution: *Use only one Form 4684 for lines 13 through 21.*

13 Add the amounts on line 12 of all Forms 4684 · · · · · · · · · · | **13** |

14 Add the amounts on line 4 of all Forms 4684 · · · · · · · · · · · | **14** |

15 • If line 14 is **more** than line 13, enter the difference here and on Schedule D. **Do not** complete the rest of this section (see instructions).
• If line 14 is **less** than line 13, enter -0- here and go to line 16.
• If line 14 is **equal** to line 13, enter -0- here. **Do not** complete the rest of this section. | **15** |

16 If line 14 is **less** than line 13, enter the difference · · · · · · · · · | **16** |

17 Add the amounts on line 12 of all Forms 4684 on which you entered -0- on line 11 · · · · · · · | **17** |

18 Is line 17 less than line 16?

☐ **No.** Stop. Enter the amount from line 16 on Schedule A (Form 1040), line 19, or Schedule A (Form 1040NR), line 8. Estates and trusts, enter the amount from line 16 on the "Other deductions" line of your tax return.

☐ **Yes.** Subtract line 17 from line 16. | **18** |

19 Enter 10% of your adjusted gross income from Form 1040, line 38, or Form 1040NR, line 36. Estates and trusts, see instructions · | **19** |

20 Subtract line 19 from line 18. If zero or less, enter -0- · · · · · · · · · · · · · | **20** |

21 Add lines 17 and 20. Also enter the result on Schedule A (Form 1040), line 19, or Schedule A (Form 1040NR), line 8. Estates and trusts, enter the result on the "Other deductions" line of your tax return · · · · · · | **21** |

For Paperwork Reduction Act Notice, see page 4 of the instructions.   Cat. No. 12997O   Form **4684** (2006)

Form 4684 (2006)   Attachment Sequence No. **26**   Page **2**

Name(s) shown on tax return. Do not enter name and identifying number if shown on other side.   Identifying number

SECTION B—Business and Income-Producing Property

Part I   Casualty or Theft Gain or Loss (Use a separate Part I for each casualty or theft.)

22   Description of properties (show type, location, and date acquired for each property). Use a separate line for each property lost or damaged from the same casualty or theft.

Property **A** _____

Property **B** _____

Property **C** _____

Property **D** _____

		Properties			
		A	**B**	**C**	**D**
23	Cost or adjusted basis of each property.	23				
24	Insurance or other reimbursement (whether or not you filed a claim). See the instructions for line 3. **Note:** *If line 23 is more than line 24, skip line 25.*	24				
25	Gain from casualty or theft. If line 24 is **more** than line 23, enter the difference here and on line 32 or line 37, column (c), except as provided in the instructions for line 36. Also, skip lines 26 through 30 for that column. See the instructions for line 4 if line 24 includes insurance or other reimbursement you did not claim, or you received payment for your loss in a later tax year.	25				
26	Fair market value **before** casualty or theft	26				
27	Fair market value **after** casualty or theft.	27				
28	Subtract line 27 from line 26	28				
29	Enter the **smaller** of line 23 or line 28. **Note:** *If the property was totally destroyed by casualty or lost from theft, enter on line 29 the amount from line 23.*	29				
30	Subtract line 24 from line 29. If zero or less, enter -0-	30				
31	Casualty or theft loss. Add the amounts on line 30. Enter the total here and on line 32 **or** line 37 (see instructions).				31	

Part II   Summary of Gains and Losses (from separate Parts I)

	(a) Identify casualty or theft	(b) Losses from casualties or thefts		(c) Gains from casualties or thefts includible in income
		(i) Trade, business, rental or royalty property	*(ii)* Income-producing and employee property	

Casualty or Theft of Property Held One Year or Less

32	_____	( )	( )	
		( )	( )	
33	Totals. Add the amounts on line 32	33 (	) (	)
34	Combine line 33, columns (b)(i) and (c). Enter the net gain or (loss) here and on Form 4797, line 14. If Form 4797 is not otherwise required, see instructions			34
35	Enter the amount from line 33, column (b)(ii) here. Individuals, enter the amount from income-producing property on Schedule A (Form 1040), line 27, or Schedule A (Form 1040NR), line 16, and enter the amount from property used as an employee on Schedule A (Form 1040), line 22, or Schedule A (Form 1040NR), line 11. Estates and trusts, partnerships, and S corporations, see instructions.			35

Casualty or Theft of Property Held More Than One Year

36	Casualty or theft gains from Form 4797, line 32			36
37	_____	( )	( )	
		( )	( )	
38	Total losses. Add amounts on line 37, columns (b)(i) and (b)(ii)	38 (	) (	)
39	Total gains. Add lines 36 and 37, column (c)			39
40	Add amounts on line 38, columns (b)(i) and (b)(ii)			40

41   If the loss on line 40 is **more** than the gain on line 39:

  a Combine line 38, column (b)(i) and line 39, and enter the net gain or (loss) here. Partnerships (except electing large partnerships) and S corporations, see the note below. All others, enter this amount on Form 4797, line 14. If Form 4797 is not otherwise required, see instructions · · · · · · · · · ·   **41a**

  b Enter the amount from line 38, column (b)(ii) here. Individuals, enter the amount from income-producing property on Schedule A (Form 1040), line 27, or Schedule A (Form 1040NR), line 16, and enter the amount from property used as an employee on Schedule A (Form 1040), line 22 or Schedule A (Form 1040NR), line 11. Estates and trusts, enter on the "Other deductions" line of your tax return. Partnerships (except electing large partnerships) and S corporations, see the note below. Electing large partnerships, enter on Form 1065-B, Part II, line 11   **41b**

42   If the loss on line 40 is **less** than or **equal** to the gain on line 39, combine lines 39 and 40 and enter here. Partnerships (except electing large partnerships), see the note below. All others, enter this amount on Form 4797, line 3 · · · ·   **42**

  Note: *Partnerships, enter the amount from line 41a, 41b, or line 42 on Form 1065, Schedule K, line 11. S corporations, enter the amount from line 41a or 41b on Form 1120S, Schedule K, line 10.*

Form **4684** (2006)

Form **4797**		**Sales of Business Property**			OMB No. 1545-0184
		(Also Involuntary Conversions and Recapture Amounts Under Sections 179 and 280F(b)(2))			20**06**
Department of the Treasury Internal Revenue Service (99)		▶Attach to your tax return. ▶See separate instructions.			Attachment Sequence No. **27**

Name(s) shown on return	Identifying number

1 Enter the gross proceeds from sales or exchanges reported to you for 2006 on Form(s) 1099-B or 1099-S (or substitute statement) that you are including on line 2, 10, or 20 (see instructions) . . . . | **1**

Part I **Sales or Exchanges of Property Used in a Trade or Business and Involuntary Conversions From Other Than Casualty or Theft—Most Property Held More Than 1 Year** (see instructions)

(a) Description of property	**(b)** Date acquired (mo., day, yr.)	**(c)** Date sold (mo., day, yr.)	**(d)** Gross sales price	**(e)** Depreciation allowed or allowable since acquisition	**(f)** Cost or other basis, plus improvements and expense of sale	**(g)** Gain or (loss) Subtract (f) from the sum of (d) and (e)
2						

3	Gain, if any, from Form 4684, line 42	**3**	
4	Section 1231 gain from installment sales from Form 6252, line 26 or 37	**4**	
5	Section 1231 gain or (loss) from like-kind exchanges from Form 8824	**5**	
6	Gain, if any, from line 32, from other than casualty or theft	**6**	
7	Combine lines 2 through 6. Enter the gain or (loss) here and on the appropriate line as follows:	**7**	

Partnerships (except electing large partnerships) and S corporations. Report the gain or (loss) following the instructions for Form 1065, Schedule K, line 10, or Form 1120S, Schedule K, line 9. Skip lines 8, 9, 11, and 12 below.

Individuals, partners, S corporation shareholders, and all others. If line 7 is zero or a loss, enter the amount from line 7 on line 11 below and skip lines 8 and 9. If line 7 is a gain and you did not have any prior year section 1231 losses, or they were recaptured in an earlier year, enter the gain from line 7 as a long-term capital gain on the Schedule D filed with your return and skip lines 8, 9, 11, and 12 below.

8	Nonrecaptured net section 1231 losses from prior years (see instructions)	**8**	
9	Subtract line 8 from line 7. If zero or less, enter -0-. If line 9 is zero, enter the gain from line 7 on line 12 below. If line 9 is more than zero, enter the amount from line 8 on line 12 below and enter the gain from line 9 as a long-term capital gain on the Schedule D filed with your return (see instructions)	**9**	

Part II **Ordinary Gains and Losses** (see instructions)

10 Ordinary gains and losses not included on lines 11 through 16 (include property held 1 year or less):

11	Loss, if any, from line 7.	**11**	( )
12	Gain, if any, from line 7 or amount from line 8, if applicable	**12**	
13	Gain, if any, from line 31	**13**	
14	Net gain or (loss) from Form 4684, lines 34 and 41a	**14**	
15	Ordinary gain from installment sales from Form 6252, line 25 or 36	**15**	
16	Ordinary gain or (loss) from like-kind exchanges from Form 8824	**16**	
17	Combine lines 10 through 16	**17**	

18 For all except individual returns, enter the amount from line 17 on the appropriate line of your return and skip lines a and b below. For individual returns, complete lines a and b below:

a If the loss on line 11 includes a loss from Form 4684, line 38, column (b)(ii), enter that part of the loss here. Enter the part of the loss from income-producing property on Schedule A (Form 1040), line 27, and the part of the loss from property used as an employee on Schedule A (Form 1040), line 22. Identify as from "Form 4797, line 18a." See instructions . . . . | **18a**

b Redetermine the gain or (loss) on line 17 excluding the loss, if any, on line 18a. Enter here and on Form 1040, line 14 . . . . | **18b**

For Paperwork Reduction Act Notice, see separate instructions.   Cat. No. 13086I   Form **4797** (2006)

Form 4797 (2006)   Page **2**

Part III **Gain From Disposition of Property Under Sections 1245, 1250, 1252, 1254, and 1255** (see instructions)

19	(a) Description of section 1245, 1250, 1252, 1254, or 1255 property:	(b) Date acquired (mo., day, yr.)	(c) Date sold (mo., day, yr.)
A			
B			
C			
D			

	These columns relate to the properties on lines 19A through 19D. ▶		Property A	Property B	Property C	Property D
20	Gross sales price (**Note:** *See line 1 before completing.*)	20				
21	Cost or other basis plus expense of sale	21				
22	Depreciation (or depletion) allowed or allowable	22				
23	Adjusted basis. Subtract line 22 from line 21	23				
24	Total gain. Subtract line 23 from line 20	24				
25	**If section 1245 property:**					
a	Depreciation allowed or allowable from line 22	25a				
b	Enter the **smaller** of line 24 or 25a	25b				
26	**If section 1250 property:** If straight line depreciation was used, enter -0- on line 26g, except for a corporation subject to section 291.					
a	Additional depreciation after 1975 (see instructions)	26a				
b	Applicable percentage multiplied by the **smaller** of line 24 or line 26a (see instructions)	26b				
c	Subtract line 26a from line 24. If residential rental property **or** line 24 is not more than line 26a, skip lines 26d and 26e	26c				
d	Additional depreciation after 1969 and before 1976	26d				
e	Enter the **smaller** of line 26c or 26d	26e				
f	Section 291 amount (corporations only)	26f				
g	Add lines 26b, 26e, and 26f	26g				
27	**If section 1252 property:** Skip this section if you did not dispose of farmland or if this form is being completed for a partnership (other than an electing large partnership).					
a	Soil, water, and land clearing expenses	27a				
b	Line 27a multiplied by applicable percentage (see instructions)	27b				
c	Enter the **smaller** of line 24 or 27b	27c				
28	**If section 1254 property:**					
a	Intangible drilling and development costs, expenditures for development of mines and other natural deposits, and mining exploration costs (see instructions)	28a				
b	Enter the **smaller** of line 24 or 28a	28b				
29	**If section 1255 property:**					
a	Applicable percentage of payments excluded from income under section 126 (see instructions)	29a				
b	Enter the **smaller** of line 24 or 29a (see instructions)	29b				

Summary of Part III Gains. Complete property columns A through D through line 29b before going to line 30.

30	Total gains for all properties. Add property columns A through D, line 24	30	
31	Add property columns A through D, lines 25b, 26g, 27c, 28b, and 29b. Enter here and on line 13	31	
32	Subtract line 31 from line 30. Enter the portion from casualty or theft on Form 4684, line 36. Enter the portion from other than casualty or theft on Form 4797, line 6	32	

Part IV **Recapture Amounts Under Sections 179 and 280F(b)(2) When Business Use Drops to 50% or Less** (see instructions)

			(a) Section 179	(b) Section 280F(b)(2)
33	Section 179 expense deduction or depreciation allowable in prior years	33		
34	Recomputed depreciation (see instructions)	34		
35	Recapture amount. Subtract line 34 from line 33. See the instructions for where to report	35		

Form **4797** (2006)

Form **8829**

Department of the Treasury
Internal Revenue Service (99)

Expenses for Business Use of Your Home

▶ File only with Schedule C (Form 1040). Use a separate Form 8829 for each home you used for business during the year.

▶ See separate instructions.

OMB No. 1545-0074

2007

Attachment
Sequence No. **66**

Name(s) of proprietor(s)

Your social security number

Part I Part of Your Home Used for Business

1	Area used regularly and exclusively for business, regularly for daycare, or for storage of inventory or product samples (see instructions)	**1**	
2	Total area of home	**2**	
3	Divide line 1 by line 2. Enter the result as a percentage	**3**	%

For daycare facilities not used exclusively for business, go to line 4. All others go to line 7.

4	Multiply days used for daycare during year by hours used per day	**4**		hr.
5	Total hours available for use during the year (365 days × 24 hours) (see instructions)	**5**	8,760	hr.
6	Divide line 4 by line 5. Enter the result as a decimal amount	**6**	.	
7	Business percentage. For daycare facilities not used exclusively for business, multiply line 6 by line 3 (enter the result as a percentage). All others, enter the amount from line 3 ▶	**7**		%

Part II Figure Your Allowable Deduction

8	Enter the amount from Schedule C, line 29, **plus** any net gain or (loss) derived from the business use of your home and shown on Schedule D or Form 4797. If more than one place of business, see instructions		**8**	

See instructions for columns (a) and (b) before completing lines 9–21.

		(a) Direct expenses	(b) Indirect expenses		
9	Casualty losses (see instructions)	**9**			
10	Deductible mortgage interest (see instructions)	**10**			
11	Real estate taxes (see instructions)	**11**			
12	Add lines 9, 10, and 11	**12**			
13	Multiply line 12, column (b) by line 7		**13**		
14	Add line 12, column (a) and line 13			**14**	
15	Subtract line 14 from line 8. If zero or less, enter -0-			**15**	
16	Excess mortgage interest (see instructions)	**16**			
17	Insurance	**17**			
18	Rent	**18**			
19	Repairs and maintenance	**19**			
20	Utilities	**20**			
21	Other expenses (see instructions)	**21**			
22	Add lines 16 through 21	**22**			
23	Multiply line 22, column (b) by line 7		**23**		
24	Carryover of operating expenses from 2006 Form 8829, line 42		**24**		
25	Add line 22 in column (a), line 23, and line 24			**25**	
26	Allowable operating expenses. Enter the **smaller** of line 15 or line 25			**26**	
27	Limit on excess casualty losses and depreciation. Subtract line 26 from line 15			**27**	
28	Excess casualty losses (see instructions)		**28**		
29	Depreciation of your home from Part III below		**29**		
30	Carryover of excess casualty losses and depreciation from 2006 Form 8829, line 43		**30**		
31	Add lines 28 through 30			**31**	
32	Allowable excess casualty losses and depreciation. Enter the **smaller** of line 27 or line 31			**32**	
33	Add lines 14, 26, and 32			**33**	
34	Casualty loss portion, if any, from lines 14 and 32. Carry amount to **Form 4684,** Section B			**34**	
35	Allowable expenses for business use of your home. Subtract line 34 from line 33. Enter here and on Schedule C, line 30. If your home was used for more than one business, see instructions ▶			**35**	

Part III Depreciation of Your Home

36	Enter the **smaller** of your home's adjusted basis or its fair market value (see instructions)	**36**	
37	Value of land included on line 36	**37**	
38	Basis of building. Subtract line 37 from line 36	**38**	
39	Business basis of building. Multiply line 38 by line 7	**39**	
40	Depreciation percentage (see instructions)	**40**	%
41	Depreciation allowable (see instructions). Multiply line 39 by line 40. Enter here and on line 29 above	**41**	

Part IV Carryover of Unallowed Expenses to 2008

42	Operating expenses. Subtract line 26 from line 25. If less than zero, enter -0-	**42**	
43	Excess casualty losses and depreciation. Subtract line 32 from line 31. If less than zero, enter -0-	**43**	

For Paperwork Reduction Act Notice, see page 4 of separate instructions.   Cat. No. 13232M   Form **8829** (2007)

 Printed on recycled paper

Form 8824

Department of the Treasury
Internal Revenue Service

Like-Kind Exchanges

(and section 1043 conflict-of-interest sales)

▶ **Attach to your tax return.**

OMB No. 1545-1190

20**06**

Attachment
Sequence No. **109**

Name(s) shown on tax return

Identifying number

Part I   Information on the Like-Kind Exchange

Note: *If the property described on line 1 or line 2 is real or personal property located outside the United States, indicate the country.*

1   Description of like-kind property given up ▶ ....

2   Description of like-kind property received ▶ ....

3 Date like-kind property given up was originally acquired (month, day, year)	**3**	/ /
4 Date you actually transferred your property to other party (month, day, year)	**4**	/ /
5 Date like-kind property you received was identified by written notice to another party (month, day, year). See instructions for 45-day written notice requirement	**5**	/ /
6 Date you actually received the like-kind property from other party (month, day, year). See instructions	**6**	/ /

7   Was the exchange of the property given up or received made with a related party, either directly or indirectly (such as through an intermediary)? See instructions. If "Yes," complete Part II. If "No," go to Part III   . . . .   ☐Yes ☐No

Part II   Related Party Exchange Information

8

Name of related party	Relationship to you	Related party's identifying number

Address (no., street, and apt., room, or suite no., city or town, state, and ZIP code)

9   During this tax year (and before the date that is 2 years after the last transfer of property that was part of the exchange), did the related party directly or indirectly (such as through an intermediary) sell or dispose of any part of the like-kind property received from you in the exchange? . . . .   ☐Yes ☐No

10   During this tax year (and before the date that is 2 years after the last transfer of property that was part of the exchange), did you sell or dispose of any part of the like-kind property you received? . . . .   ☐Yes ☐No

*If both lines 9 and 10 are "No" and this is the year of the exchange, go to Part III. If both lines 9 and 10 are "No" and this is **not** the year of the exchange, stop here. If either line 9 or line 10 is "Yes," complete Part III and report on this year's tax return the deferred gain or (loss) from line 24 **unless** one of the exceptions on line 11 applies.*

11   If one of the exceptions below applies to the disposition, check the applicable box:

a ☐ The disposition was after the death of either of the related parties.

b ☐ The disposition was an involuntary conversion, and the threat of conversion occurred after the exchange.

c ☐ You can establish to the satisfaction of the IRS that neither the exchange nor the disposition had tax avoidance as its principal purpose. If this box is checked, attach an explanation (see instructions).

For Paperwork Reduction Act Notice, see page 5.   Cat. No. 12311A   Form **8824** (2006)

Form 8824 (2006)   Page **2**

Name(s) shown on tax return. Do not enter name and social security number if shown on other side. | Your social security number

Part III   Realized Gain or (Loss), Recognized Gain, and Basis of Like-Kind Property Received

Caution: *If you transferred and received (a) more than one group of like-kind properties or (b) cash or other (not like-kind) property, see Reporting of multi-asset exchanges in the instructions.*

Note: *Complete lines 12 through 14 only if you gave up property that was not like-kind. Otherwise, go to line 15.*

12	Fair market value (FMV) of other property given up	**12**
13	Adjusted basis of other property given up	**13**
14	Gain or (loss) recognized on other property given up. Subtract line 13 from line 12. Report the gain or (loss) in the same manner as if the exchange had been a sale	**14**
	Caution: *If the property given up was used previously or partly as a home, see Property used as home in the instructions.*	
15	Cash received, FMV of other property received, plus net liabilities assumed by other party, reduced (but not below zero) by any exchange expenses you incurred (see instructions)	**15**
16	FMV of like-kind property you received	**16**
17	Add lines 15 and 16	**17**
18	Adjusted basis of like-kind property you gave up, net amounts paid to other party, plus any exchange expenses **not** used on line 15 (see instructions)	**18**
19	**Realized gain or (loss).** Subtract line 18 from line 17	**19**
20	Enter the smaller of line 15 or line 19, but not less than zero	**20**
21	Ordinary income under recapture rules. Enter here and on Form 4797, line 16 (see instructions)	**21**
22	Subtract line 21 from line 20. If zero or less, enter -0-. If more than zero, enter here and on Schedule D or Form 4797, unless the installment method applies (see instructions)	**22**
23	**Recognized gain.** Add lines 21 and 22	**23**
24	Deferred gain or (loss). Subtract line 23 from line 19. If a related party exchange, see instructions	**24**
25	**Basis of like-kind property received.** Subtract line 15 from the sum of lines 18 and 23	**25**

Part IV   Deferral of Gain From Section 1043 Conflict-of-Interest Sales

Note: *This part is to be used only by officers or employees of the executive branch of the Federal Government for reporting nonrecognition of gain under section 1043 on the sale of property to comply with the conflict-of-interest requirements. This part can be used only if the cost of the replacement property is more than the basis of the divested property.*

26	Enter the number from the upper right corner of your certificate of divestiture. (**Do not** attach a copy of your certificate. Keep the certificate with your records.). ▶	
27	Description of divested property ▶	
28	Description of replacement property ▶	
29	Date divested property was sold (month, day, year)	**29** / /
30	Sales price of divested property (see instructions)	**30**
31	Basis of divested property	**31**
32	**Realized gain.** Subtract line 31 from line 30	**32**
33	Cost of replacement property purchased within 60 days after date of sale	**33**
34	Subtract line 33 from line 30. If zero or less, enter -0-	**34**
35	Ordinary income under recapture rules. Enter here and on Form 4797, line 10 (see instructions)	**35**
36	Subtract line 35 from line 34. If zero or less, enter -0-. If more than zero, enter here and on Schedule D or Form 4797 (see instructions)	**36**
37	**Deferred gain.** Subtract the sum of lines 35 and 36 from line 32	**37**
38	**Basis of replacement property.** Subtract line 37 from line 33	**38**

Form **8824** (2006)

Glossary

(All terms are defined below as they are used in this book.)

A

Accelerated Depreciation—Depreciation method in which greater deductions are allowed in the early years of an item's recovery period.

Accounting—Tracking your self-employment income and expenses

Accrual—Method of accounting which recognizes income as it is earned and expenses when they are incurred.

Actual Expenses—Expenses associated with the cost of operating a vehicle for business purposes.

AGI—Adjusted Gross Income—A taxpayer's gross income minus deductions.

Amended Tax Return—(1040x) Filed to correct an error made on a previously filed return.

Asset—Property used in the business (i.e. equipment) having a useful life of at least one year.

Audit—Verification of income and expenses by inspection of your business and personal records.

B

Bad Debt—When income has been accounted for, but is unable to be received.

Basis—Typically the cost of an item. This amount may be increased by sales tax and improvements. It may be decreased by depreciation, deductions, credits, and insurance.

Business—Venture carried out with the intent of making profit . . . or one which continues to profit.

Business Entity—How a business operates. Business License – Permit issued locally for business operations.

C

Capital Gain—Income received on the sale of an asset above the item's adjusted basis.

Carry-Overs—Generally, amounts you were unable to deduct this year which may be deducted in future years.

Cash—Method of accounting which recognizes income as it is received and expenses when money is spent.

Class Life—The recovery period used for the depreciation of business assets.

Cost of Goods Sold—Amount paid by the business for inventory which sold during the tax year.

CPA—Certified Public Accountant—Most highly qualified of all accounting professionals.

D

Deduction—Amount which may be used to offset a taxpayer's gross income in order to arrive at his taxable income.

Depreciation—The value of an item is able to be deducted incrementally over a set number of years, called class life.

Direct Expense—An expense directly associated with the business portion of the home.

E

Earned Income—Any income earned by the taxpayer through wages, tips, salaries, or self-employment income.

EIN—Employer Identification Number. A number assigned by the IRS to a business. Necessary if you hire employees.

Employee—A worker who is under the control of the business owner for direction in exchange for pay.

Estimated Taxes—Quarterly payments made to the IRS for anticipated tax liability.

Expense—Cost incurred by the business.

F

Fair Market Value—Amount of money which would change hands for the sale of goods or equipment under the current market.
Federal Income Tax—Tax paid to the federal government based on income.
FICA—Federal Insurance Contributions Act—Comprised of Social Security and Medicare taxes.
FUTA—Federal Unemployment Tax Act.

G

Gross Income—A taxpayer's total income from all sources before any deductions or exemptions.

H

Home Office—Portion of tax payer's primary residence which is used regularly and exclusively for business purposes.

I

Independent Contractor—A worker who controls how and when work will be performed.
Indirect Expenses—Costs pertaining to the entire home, not just the business percentage of it.
Interest—Amount paid to others for the privilege of borrowing money.
Inventory—Goods, or raw materials that will become goods, a business has on hand for sale to customers.
Investment—Money spent to acquire an asset.
IRC—Internal Revenue Code—see tax code
IRS—Internal Revenue Service—Agency which is part of the U.S. Treasury Department. The IRS defines and enforces the Internal Revenue Code.
Itemized Deductions—Expenses allowed in place of the standard deduction. (i.e. mortgage interest, medical expenses, and charitable donations.)

L

Liability—Money owed by a business to others.

Listed Property—Assets used in business which the IRS believes have the potential for personal use. Therefore, the IRS requires special record keeping for such items.

M

MACRS Depreciation—Modified Accelerated Cost Recovery System—System of depreciation used for property purchased after 1986.

N

Net Income—Profit remaining after expenses and other deductions.

NOL—Net Operating Loss—The amount the expenses of a business exceed its income.

O

Ordinary Income—Any earned Income.

P

Payroll Taxes—Income taxes, Medicare, and Social Security amounts withheld from an employee's earnings.

Penalties—Fines imposed by the IRS

Personal Property—Any item of value except for real-estate.

Personal Property Taxes—Tax imposed on personal property.

Prorate—To split the cost of an item between multiple tax years.

R

Real Property—Real estate

Recapture—During the sale of an asset, the amount taxed at ordinary tax rates based on the amount of depreciation or deductions previously taken on the item.

Refund—Money owed to the taxpayer due to overpayment.

S

Sales Tax—Tax imposed on the sale of goods.

Section 1231 Property—Real property or depreciable personal property. This property must be used in a trade or business and held longer than one year.

Section 1245 Property—Includes any property that is or has been given an allowance for depreciation or amortization and is personal property.

Self-Employed—Taxpayer who works in his own business.

Self-Employment Taxes—Social Security and Medicare taxes imposed on self-employment income.

SMR—Standard Mileage Rate—Amount you may deduct for each business mile driven.

Standard Deduction—Amount Congress allows an individual taxpayer to exclude from their gross income without having to itemize and account for certain allowable deductions.

Straight-Line Depreciation—Equal deductions allowed on business assets over a specified number of years.

Subpoena—Legally enforceable order.

T

Tangible Personal Property—Personal property which is physically moveable.

Tax Code—Set of laws written by Congress mandating how we are taxed.

Tax Credit—Amount allowed to offset tax liability dollar for dollar.

Tax Liability—Amount a tax payer owes.

Tax Professional—Expert working in the field of taxes.

Tax Rate—Percentage of tax typically changing at different income levels.
Treasury Regulations—Interpretations of the tax code.

U

Unearned Income—Income received from investments.

W

Wages—Amounts paid to employees as compensation for work.
Withholding—Amount held from an employee's paycheck to cover his payroll taxes.

Index

CPSIA information can be obtained
at www.ICGtesting.com
Printed in the USA
BVHW071853060620
580740BV00006B/272

9 780979 632808